Rebellion
in a High School

Arthur L. Stinchcombe was born in Clare County, Michigan, and studied at the University of California, Berkeley. He is the author of many articles in sociological journals and is now Professor of Sociology at the University of California, Berkeley.

Rebellion in a High School

ARTHUR L. STINCHCOMBE

Chicago QUADRANGLE BOOKS

REBELLION IN A HIGH SCHOOL. Copyright © 1964 by
Arthur L. Stinchcombe. First published 1964 by Quadrangle
Books, Inc.

Second Printing and first QUADRANGLE PAPERBACK
edition published 1969 by Quadrangle Books, Inc., 12 East
Delaware Place, Chicago 60611. Manufactured in the United
States of America.

Preface

Probably most people who have not tried to write a long piece of intellectual work feel, as I used to, that acknowledgments are mostly cant and ritual. But it is, as I have found out, virtually impossible to do a sustained intellectual work without both social support and criticism, suggestion, and help. It is also actually the case that those who help do not produce the errors, omissions, faults of writing, or inanities of thought that remain.

My most substantial debts are to my dissertation committee, Philip Selznick, S. M. Lipset, and Frederic Lilge, and to my colleague, James S. Coleman. They have substantially shortened the results presented here by advising me to omit shoddier sections, advice I probably would not have taken from anyone else but which, I think, substantially improved the work. James S. Coleman did a very careful critical reading, suggested many ideas, provided me with data, and suggested extremely useful interview questions. Amitai Etzioni read the manuscript when I thought I had finished, and showed me that I had not.

v

Several people decisively influenced the intellectual foundations of the research, but are not represented in footnotes in accordance with their importance. Philip Selznick, Erving Goffman, Dorothy and William Smith, and Talcott Parsons all had very great impact on the ideas presented here when they were most ambiguous and fuzzy, without being citable for specific hypotheses. Warren Hagstrom and Martin Trow gave detailed attention and criticism to the Appendix on Method. John Walton and my wife are responsible for whatever clarity finally got into the writing.

Lois Hagstrom did the key punching of the interviews in a careful and intelligent manner, and is primarily responsible for my confidence that the answers I analyzed are the answers that appeared on the questionnaires. Myra O'Brien typed the manuscript and uncovered a number of errors and clumsy passages in the writing.

I was supported during the work by a research fellowship from the Haynes Foundation, by the United States Government under Public Law 550, and by my wife's fantastically good management of narrow resources. I was also supported during the last phases by salary from Johns Hopkins University, whose policy of starting the salary year in July deserves imitation. The costs of administering the survey and of part of the IBM work were borne by a grant from the Committee on Research of the University of California.

The obligation of any survey researcher to his respondents is obvious, but my obligation to the school studied extends beyond this. The administration and teaching staff of the school were exceptionally co-operative in providing me with help of all sorts, from permission to visit classes to the use of school time for the survey, from access to school records to friendly encouragement. And their participation in the formulation of the substance of the argument is probably more than they will be able to recognize, since it is now cloaked in sociological jargon and statistical tables. I became quite suspicious of any hypothesis that was never formulated, in one guise or another, by at least one of the teachers or administrators of the school, and many were suggested by them.

I would like to thank Doubleday and Company and T. H. Marshall for permission to quote from his *Class, Citizenship, and Social Development* at the beginning of Chapter 7. Basic Books, John Wiley and Sons, *The American Sociological Review*, The Free Press of Glencoe, John Day and Company, Imago, Farrar Straus and Company, and the Macmillan Company have kindly granted permission to quote passages from works published by them, as noted in citations.

Finally, a note on pronouns. I have used "we" whenever the reference is to an intellectual process which is an inherent part of the argument, in which the reader must participate if he is to judge adequately the truth of what is said. I have used "I" whenever the reference is to an arbitrary personal decision, which could as well have been made some other way, or for an intellectual process which has a large element of personal judgment with little evidence on which to base it. The "I" to "we" ratio in a chapter or argument is perhaps a measure of the degree of confidence I myself have in the results.

A. L. S.

Baltimore, Maryland
May 1964

Contents

Rebellion
in a High School

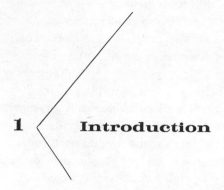

1 Introduction

DELINQUENCY AND HIGH SCHOOL REBELLION

The student-teacher relation in high school is one of the few authority relations in modern society whose maintainence is consistently problematic. Though authority everywhere frequently meets with lack of enthusiasm by subordinates, it is not often openly flouted and insulted. Though authorities everywhere have difficulty persuading subordinates to be devoted to the goals of organizations, they only rarely have difficulty carrying on orderly social intercourse. It is consistently problematic whether orderly social intercourse will take place in classrooms.

The deviant behavior that creates this problem occurs *where the norms are socially and psychologically present.* An active representative of the high school is in the room when the "delinquent acts" are committed. It is a negative response to authorities, not deviant behavior in general,

1

that creates the discipline problem in high schools. Of course, other delinquencies may also have some of this character; all deviant behavior that is rooted in "taking a dare" derives its excitement from the psychological presence of norms.

That is, high school rebellion is *flouting* rules rather than *evading* rules. There is a difference between a high school student who drinks with a gang of boys in a car on a country road, and one who drinks *and then* comes to a school dance. The first is a problem of delinquency; the second a problem of orderly social intercourse. Much, perhaps most, adolescent (and adult) "delinquent behavior" can be explained by the failure of norms to be socially and psychologically present in the situation where the delinquent behavior occurs.[1] But such an argument cannot explain the differential conformity with authorities who are in the room, nor does it provide a clue to the vivid *impiety* that high school teachers confront.

High school rebellion involves expression of alienation from socially present authorities; it may thus be called "expressive alienation." The contention here is that "rebellion" is a manifestation of "expressive alienation," and that high school rebellion has an emotional quality of hatred or sullenness.[2] Other deviant behavior may have the emotional quality of cynicism, or indifference to rules, or ignorance of correct behavior. Cynicism, indifference, indignation, or ideological disagreement with norms are other forms of alienation, or ideological disagreement with norms are other forms of alienation, different in emotional tone. The adjective "expressive" should connote some of the special quality of alienation from high school authority, especially its responsive, non-ideological, unorganized, and impulsive character.

Two recent descriptions of the psychological quality of de-

1. See especially F. Ivan Nye, *Family Relationships and Delinquent Behavior* (New York: John Wiley, 1958), pp. 154-158.
2. Cf. Fritz Redl and David Wineman, *Children Who Hate* (Glencoe: The Free Press, 1951).

linquents[3] may be abstracted to give an ideal-typical description of "expressive alienation."

1. It is non-utilitarian. No long-run goals, accomplishments, or rewards are necessary to motivate such deviance. Long-run goals may, of course, be supplied by institutionalization of juvenile delinquency, which links rebelliousness to adult criminal organizations and provides careers for delinquent leadership. But *as classroom rebellion* it does not require such institutionalization.[4]

2. It is malicious and negativistic, involving hatred of "nice" people and a negative attitude toward conformity in general.

3. It involves short-run hedonism. Specifically:

 (a) Activities are rejected when frustration must be borne for the sake of achieving some goal.

 (b) Activities whose motivation involves an image of a personal future tend not to be undertaken.

 (c) Activities which sublimate impulses into "respectable" and disciplined behavior are rejected in favor of immediate gratifications.

 (d) Fear of failure leads to rejection of activity involving the risk of failure.

 (e) Interference with current "fun" by an authoritative adult (enforcing rules or setting

3. *Ibid.*, pp. 240-242 (section entitled "Beyond the Reach of Education"), and Albert K. Cohen, *Delinquent Boys* (Glencoe: The Free Press, 1955), pp. 25-31.
4. Though long-run goals can be added to the delinquent subculture, this is irrelevant to recruitment to these cultures. It is especially irrelevant to classroom rebellion, which cannot earn its way. For a different view, see John I. Kitsuse and David C. Dietricke, "Delinquent Boys: A Critique," *American Sociological Review*, Vol. 24 (April 1959), pp. 208-215. "The delinquents whose activities are organized by a delinquent subculture are attending to more serious enterprises. There is no absence of rational, calculated, utilitarian behavior among delinquent gangs, as they exist today." (p. 213.)

goals) is interpreted as a hostile move, even if the rules and goals in themselves are considered legitimate by the delinquents.

4. It emphasizes group autonomy from adult interference on principle. As in other deviant social movements, connection with or loyalty to any section of the legitimate (in this case, adult) order is viewed with suspicion.

The first major hypothesis, then, is that students who are rebellious in high school are likely to have a psychological set with the above characteristics: *high school rebellion is part of a complex of attitudes toward psychologically present authority, characterized by non-utilitarianism, negativism, short-run hedonism, and emphasis on group autonomy.* But this specific kind of alienation from norms is itself traceable to the social structure of the school.

◈

EXPLANATIONS OF OBEDIENCE AND REBELLION

It has often been noted that the explanation of deviance has to be an explanation of conformity. For instance, Albert K. Cohen says:

"A theory of deviant behavior not only must account for the occurrence of deviant behavior; it must also account for its failure to occur, or conformity. In fact, the explanation of one necessarily implies the explanation of the other. Therefore 'the sociology of deviant behavior' is elliptical for 'the sociology of deviant behavior and conformity'; it includes the explanation of the prevention, reduction and elimination of deviant behavior."[5]

This study attempts to explain disobedience (and conse-

5. *Sociology Today*, edited by R. K. Merton, *et al.* (New York: Basic Books, 1959), pp. 463-464.

quently obedience) among high school students. Since the theory of obedience to authority has developed separately from the theory of adolescent rebellion, we must first discuss the relation between these theories.

The theory of obedience is most fully developed by Max Weber in his treatment of the forms of authority.[6] Each of Weber's three types of authority (bureaucratic, charismatic, and traditional) is described by specifying two main variables: (a) the type of control by authorities over the future status of subordinates, and (b) the type of commitment to symbols of legitimacy common among subordinates.

For instance, bureaucratic authority involves career commitment by the official, control of promotion by superiors on the basis of qualifications, and salary in keeping with the status of the office rather than need or family status. Further, the basis of legitimacy of bureaucratic authority is the loyalty of subordinates to a codified and rationalized body of rules and laws.[7]

We are not here concerned with the classification of types of authority, nor with judging which type would be more effective for student-teacher relations. But Weber's emphasis on control of future status suggests the second basic hypothesis of this study. *We hold that high school rebellion,* and expressive alienation, *occurs when future status is not clearly related to present performance.* When a student realizes that he does not achieve status increment from improved current performance, current performance loses

6. Max Weber, *The Theory of Social and Economic Organization* (Glencoe: The Free Press, 1947), pp. 324-363.
7. *Ibid.* Charismatic authority awards status to subordinates by arbitrary (inspired) decision by the leader. The symbol to which subordinates are loyal is the charismatic leader himself, a man especially chosen by the arbitrary will of God or History and endowed by this special choice with supernatural abilities. Traditional authority involves allocation on the basis of traditional rules (rather than either the whim of the leader or qualifications), with reward coming from the prerogatives of ascribed status (e.g., in feudalism, claims to the yield of a parcel of land). The basis of legitimacy is belief in the sacredness of traditional obligations of ascribed status.

meaning. The student becomes hedonistic because he does not visualize achievement of long-run goals through current self-restraint. He reacts negatively to a conformity that offers nothing concrete. He claims autonomy from adults because their authority does not promise him a satisfactory future.

The future, not the past, explains adolescent rebellion, contrary to the hypothesis that deviant attitudes are the result of distinctively rebel biographies. Thus Sutherland holds that deviant attitudes are learned through association with others who hold such attitudes, that biographies of deviants are characterized by wider past association with other deviants.[8] Redl and Wineman trace the set of deviant attitudes to experiences, especially lack of love, which cripple the development of the ego.[9] We hold that deviant values or crippling of the ego are traceable to differences in the futures of adolescents.

Further analysis of Weber's discussion supplies another basic hypothesis. Every organization with authority relations has *a doctrine of legitimacy* which justifies that authority. In the high school this doctrine includes beliefs about the immaturity of adolescents, and about the sharp division between behavior appropriate for adolescents and for adults. This dichotomy is expressed in a number of symbols, or badges, of adolescent and adult status.

When the symbols or badges of *adult* status are usurped by adolescents, the legitimacy of school authority is challenged. The doctrine that underlies school authority is subverted. Identification with an adult role implies[10] (especially for boys) a claim to personal and group autonomy incompatible with school authority.

8.   See Edwin H. Sutherland and D. R. Cressey, *Principles of Criminology* (5th ed.) (Philadelphia: Lippincott, 1955), pp. 77-80.
9.   *Op. cit.*
10.   Cf. Nelson Foote, "Identification as the Basis for a Theory of Motivation," *American Sociological Review*, Vol. 16 (1951), pp. 14-21.

The third hypothesis, then, is that *when the symbols of the formal school culture fail to provide a satisfactory identification with the role of adolescent, students identify with adult symbols, and expressive alienation results.*

◆

THE SOCIAL PSYCHOLOGY OF ANOMIE

The hypotheses above identify a type of lack of commitment to norms, or as it is traditionally called *"anomie"*; they then locate the social structural and cultural conditions under which anomie occurs. It remains to specify the psychological mechanisms that create the connection between the structural and cultural situation and the anomic state. The theory developed in Merton's essay on "Social Structure and Anomie" is appropriate for that purpose.[1]

Under modern conditions, all the people in certain categories are expected to aim for the same goals.[2] But some of the people in the category may be less capable of winning these goals, because they cannot get the means of success. When a person is expected to accomplish more than he can possibly accomplish, he tends to reject either the goals or the rules which limit the means, or both.

High school rebellion is an active rejection of the social world of the school. That is, it involves rejection of both the goals and the means of success, as success is defined by the school and by the labor market. The school puts all who can do algebra into a class in algebra, but those who can do

1. In *Social Theory and Social Structure* (1st ed.) (Glencoe: The Free Press, 1949), pp. 125-149.
2. Merton formulates this specifically for the American case as the expectation that all people will be successful in making money. Of course, this applies to the category of men much more than to women, and to middle class people more than to workers. But to the extent it applies to a category, it applies equally, regardless of access to the means of success. It is this *universalism* of success expectations, rather than their *universality*, that causes disproportions between goals and means.

automobile mechanics are put into that class only if they cannot do algebra. Thus the school defines talent at algebra as success, talent at auto mechanics as failure. But since we find students being rebellious, rather than apathetic, we infer that there is still enough involvement in the social world of the school to motivate activism and cause rebellion rather than apathy. It is my contention that expressive alienation, and high school rebellion, are "reaction formations" which actively reject partially internalized goals of success. That is, we will expect that *among those who are failing in school, those under the most pressure to succeed will be most rebellious,* because rebellion is a way of rejecting pressure for success.

The fourth basic hypothesis, then, is that *whenever the goals of success are strongly internalized but inaccessible, expressive alienation results.* Such goals are strongly internalized in categories of people who are expected to succeed. This refers especially to boys, and among boys, especially those from middle class families, because in our culture success is expected of boys more than of girls, and is expected more in the middle class than in the working class. Failure among middle class boys should, then, produce greater alienation than among working class boys.

◆

SUMMARY OF THE ARGUMENT

The problem of order in high schools is created by that kind of deviant behavior which occurs in the social and psychological presence of authorities. This deviant behavior involves the active expression of alienation. Students who get into trouble with school authorities therefore tend to have attitudes rejecting the school social world.

The sources of this attitude (and consequently of rebellion) are to be found in (a) strains in status allocation, (b) strains in the system of cultural symbols that makes the subordination of adolescents legitimate, and (c) the psychological strains created by standards of success that apply equally to students with different chances for success.

(a) The social structure either provides or fails to provide a sensible and appealing career pattern to the student. Whenever present activity fails to make sense by being clearly connected to future increments of status, the student tends to become expressively alienated and rebellious. The student who grasps a clear connection between current activity and future status tends to regard school authority as legitimate, and to obey. The problem of order, then, is created by the inability of the school to realistically offer any desirable status beyond high school to some of its students.

(b) The system of symbols on which school authority depends are those of age-grading, that is, symbols that distinguish adults from children and justify school authority by pointing to age differences. When these symbols fail to elicit loyalty because the student rejects the picture of himself as an adolescent, expressive alienation results.

(c) The psychological mechanism by which poor articulation between present activity and future status creates lack of commitment to symbols of adolescent status, and alienation from school authority, is the "reaction formation." That is, students who have internalized the standards of success appropriate to a category, but do not themselves have the means of success, engage in active rejection of the social world that places them in this internal conflict. Expressive alienation occurs when students replace the success orientation expected of them with active rejection of the social world of the school.

◆

THE STUDY

The hypotheses above were developed during the course of about six months of anthropological observation and exploratory survey research in a California high school. The evidence for them, presented in the rest of the book, was collected by survey techniques from the student body of the same school.

The school studied was located in a logging and sawmill town of about 4,000 population. Approximately two-thirds of the students came to the school from out of town. The small towns and rural areas from which the majority of the students came are spread over a relatively large area, requiring some of the students to travel up to 60 miles to and from school.

The logging and lumber industry on which the regional economy is based has a low skill mix, high geographical mobility, and wide dispersion of work places. The logging industry also is unbureaucratized, so that many lower middle class people are entrepreneurs who work manually in their own small businesses. This means that the social class structure has a large proportion of people in the lower ranges. But the high mobility and wide dispersion of the community prevents the formation of very tightly knit social classes. The community has a high degree of anonymity, relative isolation of the high school culture from the community culture,[3] and gives the resident the feeling of living in a city.

The state college for the region is located in the town, and the high school studied was used for the training of teachers. Consequently the role of "young adult of unspecified status hanging around the high school" was accepted easily by the students. The presence of a college with low admissions standards and limited social distinctiveness in the town also made college-going aspirations realistic even to the working class student body.

The high school has about 1,600 students in grades 9 through 12. The curriculum includes a required academic

---

3. For example, although I spent most of the year doing research in the high school, I made no attempt to work out a community role. As far as I know, no one outside the school knew or cared what I was doing.

core of English, social studies, science, and mathematics. Among the electives are academic subjects suitable for college preparation, commercial subjects pointing toward clerical work, and shop courses preparing for various manual jobs. Approximately equal teaching time is devoted to preparation for each of these three careers. Among the electives are also home economics, art, and music. Four years of physical education are required.

The typical school day for students comprises six hours of classes. Teachers are normally responsible for five hours of classes a day. Required academic classes usually number about 30 to 35 students; the electives vary around a somewhat lower average. The formal structure of the school has few features which distinguish it from other well-run American high schools.

The informal culture of the school, however, seems to have two somewhat distinctive features.[4] The sex-role differentiation, though sharper than in most schools, is quite similar to that found in other working class schools. Boys in working class schools are considerably less involved in informal school activities and segregate themselves more into single-sex groups. There is great emphasis on masculinity and on not being a "sissy."

The value climate seems to be more favorable to academic achievement than in most schools, but other characteristics of adolescent culture follow familiar patterns. Dating frequency, amount of homework done, car ownership, the predominance of athletics, all follow usual patterns.

Except for the working class, mobile, and ecologically dispersed character of the logging economy, the community context should not seriously limit the ability to generalize

4. These suggestions are based on comparisons with ten Midwestern schools studied by James S. Coleman. I asked some of the same questions he asked of the student bodies of the ten Midwestern schools, and compared the distribution of responses with his. The tabulations are not reproduced here.

from the results.[5] And except for greater emphasis on the somewhat contradictory cultures of masculinity and academic achievement, the school's structure and culture should not limit generalization.

An analysis of the methods of collecting and analyzing the survey results is presented in the Appendix on Method. Briefly, pencil and paper precoded schedules were administered by teachers in required social science classes. All schedules (including the so-called "unusable" schedules) were transferred to IBM cards for the analysis. Students absent on the day schedules were administered were not reached; otherwise a complete enumeration of the school was obtained.

Chapter 2 presents the evidence for the first hypothesis: that high school rebellion is a component of "expressive alienation," that high school rebels are hedonistic, negativistic, object to legitimate authority and status systems, and claim autonomy from adults.

In this argument we will use an index of rebellion composed of three self-reported rebellious acts: skipping school with a gang of kids, receiving a flunk notice in a non-college-preparatory class, and being sent out of class by a teacher. These three items create a partial ordering of students on the variable of rebelliousness. The construction and validity of the index is discussed in the Appendix on Method.

In Chapters 3 and 4 argument and evidence are presented for the "articulation hypothesis" which holds that the articulation of post-high school status with present academic activity produces conformity; poor articulation produces rebellion. We further argue that poor articulation produces rebellion because it produces expressive alienation. Chapter 3 demonstrates that less intelligent boys, who produce the most rebellion, do have poorer articulation of present per-

5. The absence of a vigorous adult criminal community and low development of a systematic delinquent subculture may differentiate this school from city slum schools.

formance with future status; indicators of poor articulation are also developed which can be used to make a direct test of the hypothesis. Chapter 4 offers evidence and argument to show that the hypothesis of articulation is a more valid predictor of rebellion than common sense, or the most prevalent sociological theory. First, the hypothesis is better than the common sense observation that dull boys are most rebellious, for it also predicts the incidence of rebellion and expressive alienation among girls. Next, we show that it explains the distribution of rebelliousness better than the theory of differential socialization for school life in the different social classes, which offers only a poor explanation for rebellion. Finally, the hypothesis allows us to predict expressive alienation, even when this alienation has not yet resulted in rebellious acts.

Chapter 5 turns to the cultural aspect of alienation from formal school authority. We argue that the formal organization of the school threatens the self-respect of those who do not achieve by fostering a set of symbols of the worthwhile life permeated by achievement values. Students who do not achieve tend to substitute ascriptive symbols of personal worth. They claim, in particular, rights to adult privileges, which throws them into conflict with the authority system of the school, for school authority requires the acceptance of adolescent status by the student.

Chapter 6 investigates the psychological mechanisms of the transfer of loyalty away from the school and its symbols. Some of the evidence suggests that people with different social class and sex statuses are less able to accept academic failure. If these people fail, they tend to react violently against the system that punishes their self-respect, although some of the indicators that should measure strain between achievement commitments and actual failure do not accurately predict rebellion and alienation. A few of the research problems in this area are suggested.

Chapter 7 is the conclusion. The appendices contain a

summary of, and argument for, the methodological procedures used (Appendix on Method), and a copy of The Survey Schedule (Appendix II).[6]

6.   Graphs giving more detailed data on the relation of rebellion to
social class, year in school, occupational aspirations and expectations,
curriculum choice, grade average and English class ability level are
found in Appendix II of the dissertation on which this book is based.
"Social Sources of Rebellion in a High School" (Berkeley: University
of California, 1960).

2 $\Big\langle$ The Psychological Quality of Adolescent Rebellion

The task of this chapter is to demonstrate that high school rebellion is part of a complex of attitudes toward the school environment, including short-run hedonism, negativism, alienation from school authority, and emphasis on autonomy. Though it is possible that this set of attitudes might be produced in specific situations and lead to rebellion, then be extinguished by the further course of school experience, this is not usually the case. In fact, students who have a history of rebellion in high school are much more likely than well-behaved students to have hedonistic, negativistic, alienated, and autonomous attitudes at all times. The specific hypothesis, then, is that students who have *in the past* committed rebellious acts are much more likely to hold hedonistic, negativistic, alienated, and autonomous attitudes at the time they answer the questionnaire. Presumably these attitudes have persisted for some time, and have caused rebellion in the past.

There is, first of all, a strong relation between rebellion and short-run hedonism. Next, rebellious students are neg-

15

ativistic, in that they evaluate conformity and conformists negatively. Rebellious students are alienated from school authories, believing that teachers, principals, and the leaders among students conspire among themselves to do injustice. Finally, rebels are much more likely than well-behaved students to claim rights, for themselves and for their peers, that the school is unwilling to grant.

When all of these attitudes have been shown to be related to rebellion, we will have established that "expressive alienation" is an empirical entity. That is, we will have established that high school rebellion is ordinarily a symptom of an underlying psychological state that involves hedonism, negativism, alienation from authority, and claims to autonomy. This transforms the dependent variable of the study from rebellion *per se* to expressive alienation, one of whose *symptoms* is rebellion. Later chapters will try to explain expressive alienation, rather than simply rebellion.

◆

SHORT-RUN HEDONISM

We are primarily interested in alienation from the social world of the school. Consequently, when we speak of "short-run hedonism" we mean a short-run hedonistic attitude toward that social world. All our indicators of short-run hedonism ask the student to express an attitude toward some aspect of the school. Whether or not the attitude of short-run hedonism is a character trait, and includes a short-run orientation to other social worlds, is of no concern here. It may well be that students who have a short-run attitude toward the school are disciplined workers, carefully consider the long-run problem of supporting their families, and carefully budget in order to buy cars. Likewise, negativism is only of interest here as a negative evaluation of conformity to school norms; perhaps negativistic students admire men who conform to the ideals of the world of work. A student who is alienated from school authority may have a very favorable attitude toward army officers. Students who claim autonomy from governance by school authorities may have absolutely no interest in defending the autonomy of conscience of pacifists.

In other words, the short-run hedonism relevant for us is that orientation which refuses to govern current activity by long-run goals set by the school. Negativism is used here to mean a negative attitude toward conformity with school norms; alienation from authority is alienation from school authority; a culture of autonomy is objection to the school's regulation of decisions. Our concept of "expressive alienation" is, then, an organization of attitudes toward a specific social object, the school environment. Whether or not it colors orientation to other social objects, and whether it has a long-run effect on the character structure of students, are empirical questions we will not attempt to answer.

Short-run hedonism has several aspects, any of which could serve as measures of hedonistic attitudes toward school. The short-run hedonistic attitude involves an emotional aspect: hedonistic people are bored when the meaning of the activity is expressed in long-run goals. Hedonism involves a cognitive aspect: the world is interpreted as a place in which it does not pay to sacrifice existing pleasures for uncertain future goals. Hedonism involves a failure of the imagination: future goals do not seem as real or worthwhile as current gratification.

The meaning of classroom activity is given by long-run goals. Most classes require continuous orientation to longer-run pleasures in accomplishment. Only participation classes (such as music or physical education) are consistently immediately gratifying. Consequently, boredom in classes is an index of short-run hedonism. In Table 1, the proportion of students who consider half or more of their

Table 1: Rebels are more likely to find half or more of their classes "pretty boring," among both girls and boys. Data for upper classmen.

GIRLS

Receipt of
Non-College
Flunk Notice

		Have *Not* Been Sent Out	Have Been Sent Out
		Per Cent Finding Classes Boring	
Have **Not** Skipped	No	14% (293)	* (4)
	Yes	36% (42)	* (3)
Have Skipped	No	32% (81)	* (7)
	Yes	39% (31)	* (6)
	All who have been Sent Out		25% (20)

*Too few cases for meaningful percentages.

BOYS

Receipt of
Non-College
Flunk Notice

		Have *Not* Been Sent Out	Have Been Sent Out
		Per Cent Finding Classes Boring	
Have **Not** Skipped	No	14% (207)	25% (44)
	Yes	17% (60)	39% (29)
Have Skipped	No	32% (66)	28% (46)
	Yes	28% (42)	59% (56)

classes "pretty boring" is tabulated against rebellion. It is immediately clear that rebels are more likely to be bored than are well-behaved students, but among rebels the type and amount of misbehavior makes little difference. There are no strong and consistent differences among sub-groups of rebels. Only the extreme rebels among boys, those who have received flunk notices, *and* skipped with a gang, *and* been sent out of class, show much greater tendency to boredom. About three-fifths (59 per cent) report that half or more of their classes are pretty boring.

More boys than girls report boredom: about a fifth (21 per cent) of the girls, but 27 per cent of the boys, report extensive boredom,[1] but it is only rebellious boys who are more bored than girls. About one out of seven (14 per cent) of both boys and girls who have so far been well-behaved are bored by most of their classes. But rebellious boys are both more numerous, and more likely to report boredom, than rebellious girls. These sex-differences will be discussed later.

Second, willingness to work in class depends on the student's cognitive image of the classroom in which his work yields future reward. Short-run hedonism is indicated by an inclination not to see the connection between work and future rewards. If students respond that "it doesn't matter very much how hard you work in a class — your grade is pretty much set when you first come in," this indicates a short-run hedonistic orientation of a different kind. The percentages of students responding that the statement was "Certainly True" or "Probably True" are presented in Table 2.

The sex-difference is insignificant on this question (17 per cent of girls, and 18 per cent of boys, perceiving little connection between work and grades). Yet this is not due to

1. The direct relation between sex and expressive alienation will not be tabulated separately in the tables of this chapter. The percentage alienated for boys and girls will be presented in the text.

Table 2: Rebellious students more frequently believe that work in class is not rewarded, among both girls and boys. Data for upper classmen.

GIRLS

Receipt of
Non-College
Flunk Notice

		Have Not Been Sent Out	Have Been Sent Out
		Per Cent Believing Work Not Rewarded	
Have Not Skipped	No	14% (293)	* (4)
	Yes	36% (42)	* (3)
Have Skipped	No	17% (81)	* (7)
	Yes	29% (31)	* (6)
	All who have been Sent Out		25% (20)

*Too few cases for meaningful percentages.

BOYS

Receipt of
Non-College
Flunk Notice

		Have Not Been Sent Out	Have Been Sent Out
		Per Cent Believing Work Not Rewarded	
Have Not Skipped	No	7% (207)	30% (44)
	Yes	22% (60)	31% (29)
Have Skipped	No	17% (66)	30% (46)
	Yes	24% (42)	32% (56)

lack of association between cognitive hedonism and behavioral rebellion. Since there are more rebellious boys, an attitude associated with rebellion ought normally to be also associated with sex. Those who flunk classes and those who have been sent out of class are more short-run in their orientation, among both boys and girls. But the sex-difference in behavioral rebellion is compensated by the larger proportion of girls at a given level of rebellion who have a short-run attitude on this question. For instance, 14 per cent of well-behaved girls agree that grades do not depend on work, which is twice as many as agreed among well-behaved boys.

It seems that this question also taps the orientation of short-run hedonism specifically in the classroom. Generalized lack of commitment to the school, indicated by skipping, is not strongly related to cognitive hedonism. But both types of difficulty within the classroom, flunking non-college courses and being sent out to the Attendance Office, are related to seeing the classroom as a place where work does not pay.

A third way to approach short-run hedonism is by considering the vigor of commitment to long-run goals. Attributing little importance to long-run goals will encourage an orientation to current, ephemeral gratification. Therefore, answers to the question, "How important would you say your grades were to your own satisfaction?" provide a different indicator of short-run hedonism. These answers are reported in Table 3. Again the sex-difference shows up clearly, with boys claiming much less importance for grades. The difference between the extreme rebels and the well-behaved is quite striking. Only half as many of the most rebellious boys answer that grades are important to themselves (36 per cent), as answer that way among the well-behaved boys (80 per cent).

In summary, all indications point to the greater short-run hedonism of the rebellious students. The differences between well-behaved boys and extremely rebellious boys range

Table 3: Rebels are less likely to consider grades very or quite important to their personal satisfaction, among both girls and boys. Data for upper classmen.

GIRLS

Receipt of
Non-College
Flunk Notice

		Have Not Been Sent Out	Have Been Sent Out
		Per Cent Considering Grades Important	
Have Not Skipped	No	88% (293)	* (4)
	Yes	64% (42)	* (3)
Have Skipped	No	76% (81)	* (7)
	Yes	55% (31)	* (6)
	All who have been Sent Out		55% (20)

*Too few cases for meaningful percentages.

BOYS

Receipt of
Non-College
Flunk Notice

		Have Not Been Sent Out	Have Been Sent Out
		Per Cent Considering Grades Important	
Have Not Skipped	No	80% (207)	80% (44)
	Yes	70% (60)	72% (29)
Have Skipped	No	68% (66)	50% (46)
	Yes	57% (42)	36% (56)

from 25 per cent to 45 per cent in the expected directions. In emotional reaction to situations involving sacrifice of present gratification for future satisfaction, the rebellious students are more apt to be bored. Rebellious students are less likely to connect work to the rewards that are supposed to flow from it, perceiving that grades do not depend on effort. Rebels fail to derive as much satisfaction from the long-run goals set them by the school.

At least this far, the concept of "expressive alienation" remains intact. The elements of behavioral rebellion and short-run hedonism are factually connected.

◆

NEGATIVISM

"Negativism" describes the attitude that rejects all conforming behavior, all moral attachment to legitimate institutions. The people, in particular, who have such moral attachments to the respectable world are disrespected. Not only are the rules worthless, but only a person with no backbone would follow them.

This aspect of the negativistic attitude provides an indicator of negativism. Students were asked to mark as True or False a statement that one thing wrong with the school was the number of "squares" among the students, who would rather follow all the rules than have any fun. The statement of the question unfortunately connects the attitude with short-run hedonism, but clearly the predominant element is the rejection of conformists. The distribution of answers by sex and by behavioral rebellion is reported in Table 4.

First, it is clear that negative attitudes toward conformity-in-general are more common among boys than among girls. Not only is the sex-difference substantial (32 per cent of boys and 17 per cent of girls agreeing), but well-behaved boys are considerably more likely than well-behaved girls to evaluate conformity negatively. Second, a combination

Table 4: Rebellious students, especially those with multiple offenses, find "too many squares in this school." Data for upper classmen.

GIRLS

Receipt of
Non-College
Flunk Notice

		Have *Not* Been Sent Out	Have Been Sent Out
		Per Cent Seeing Too Many Squares	
Have **Not** Skipped	No	9% (293)	* (4)
	Yes	24% (42)	* (3)
Have Skipped	No	31% (81)	* (7)
	Yes	31% (31)	* (6)
	All who have been Sent Out		50% (20)

*Too few cases for meaningful percentages.

BOYS

Receipt of
Non-College
Flunk Notice

		Have *Not* Been Sent Out	Have Been Sent Out
		Per Cent Seeing Too Many Squares	
Have **Not** Skipped	No	22% (207)	25% (44)
	Yes	20% (60)	66% (29)
Have Skipped	No	30% (66)	43% (46)
	Yes	48% (42)	52% (56)

of offenses (skipping *and* flunking, being sent out *and* skipping, etc.) is most closely related to this attitude, which is to be expected. An attitude of rejection of conformity-in-general should result in the student getting into trouble in a number of different ways.[2]

◆

ALIENATION FROM THE STATUS SYSTEM

It will be useful to reinterpret the negative reaction to authority mentioned in the original formulation of

2. Actually, though it is not relevant to the analysis, the first offense is not as closely related to negativism as we would expect; the second offense is very closely related to negativism; the third offense makes very little difference. If we fit a linear model to the above data for boys, predict the proportion negativistic in each cell, and then subtract the predicted from the actual data, we get the following picture:

Differences between actual and predicted proportion negativistic, using a linear (additive) model for prediction, boys only.

	Type of Rebellion			
	Truancy	Flunking	Classroom	Actual-Predicted
No Offense				
	No	No	No	+ 5%
One Offense				
	No	Yes	No	− 13%
	Yes	No	No	− 3%
	No	No	Yes	− 8%
Two Offenses				
	No	Yes	Yes	+ 16%
	Yes	No	Yes	0%
	Yes	Yes	No	+ 5%
Three Offenses				
	Yes	Yes	Yes	− 8%

That is, no matter whether flunking, skipping, or being sent out is considered, the first offense is less closely related to negativism (i.e., the actual proportion negativistic is lower) than we would expect if the first offense had the effect of that type of offense on the average. But each one of the second offenses is at least as closely related to negativism as we expect. The final offense doesn't make as much difference as it should on an additive assumption.

"expressive alienation." One of the aspects of this reaction is inherent in the rebellious behavior we have been using as a criterion. One way to react negatively to authority is not to obey. Another way to react negatively is to perceive the activity of the authority as illegitimate. In other words, we want to distinguish between disruption of authority relations through *disobedience,* and disruption through *disrespect.* This is, of course, a rough distinction. Disrespectful behavior is generally disobedience, and in many organizations a disrespectful attitude is punished if discovered.

In formal organizations, such as high schools, one of the central functions of authorities is to establish the status system of the organization. A status system is a socially established pattern of *judgment of persons,* with respect to their relative worth. This may be worth for doing a particular job in the organization, or may be generalized to a judgment of worth "as persons." The connection between authority and the status system means that attitudes toward the status system itself partly determine attitudes toward authorities.

A status system includes at least the following elements:

(1) A group of judges, who allocate rights and duties of the system according to their judgments of worth. For instance, the rights of access to social circles may be allocated in small communities by a relatively small group of mature middle and upper class women, according to their judgments of family background, deportment, and the like. Or employers allocate the rights and duties of employment in the labor market status system.

(2) A set of standards, more or less generally accepted, setting forth criteria of value and worth for the purposes of the judgment in question. For example, education, skill, and experience (but not race or religion in states with FEPC) are the standards most relevant in the labor market. Intellectual achievement is most important in the status system of the classroom.

(3) A recognized process according to which people present themselves for judgment. In some status systems, for example the labor market, a man need not present himself for judgment unless he wants the job. In others, such as the system of mutual visiting in a small community or the grading system of a high school, it is virtually impossible not to come up for judgment at some time or other.

(4) A set of arrangements by which the judges receive information on which to base judgment. The testing systems of schools, the recommendations of the labor market, the "rushing" of fraternities and sororities all serve this function in the relevant status systems.

(5) A set of status rewards allocated by judges. For instance, diffuse visiting rights, positions of community responsibility, and social prestige are allocated by the upper class cliques in a small community. Better pay and cleaner work are allocated by superiors in a bureaucracy.

This means that alienation from the status system can have several aspects. The judges may be held to be not applying the standards fairly; the standards may be considered illegitimate; it may be held that accidental factors prevent people from coming to the notice of the judges; it may be held that the type of information gathering used does not reveal the true worth of the person judged; or it may merely be held, without intellectual rationale, that rewards are unfairly distributed.

Since the main interest is in the alienation from authority, and since authorities play the role of judges, our indicators are chiefly of the first kind: they ask students to agree or disagree with statements that official judges allocate status unfairly. One item is of the last sort; it merely asks students to agree or disagree that statuses in student activities are unfairly distributed. A final indicator is of a slightly different kind. Students were asked to agree or disagree that most parents would feel uncomfortable coming to see a teacher or to a Parent-Teachers' Association meeting. We

Table 5: Rebels perceive teachers as unfair, among both girls and boys. Data for upper classmen.

GIRLS

Receipt of
Non-College
Flunk Notice

		Have Not Been Sent Out	Have Been Sent Out
		Per Cent Seeing Teachers Unfair	
Have Not Skipped	No	21% (293)	* (4)
	Yes	43% (42)	* (3)
Have Skipped	No	20% (81)	* (7)
	Yes	34% (31)	* (6)
		All who have been Sent Out	35% (20)

*Too few cases for meaningful percentages.

BOYS

Receipt of
Non-College
Flunk Notice

		Have Not Been Sent Out	Have Been Sent Out
		Per Cent Seeing Teachers Unfair	
Have Not Skipped	No	23% (207)	57% (44)
	Yes	25% (60)	52% (29)
Have Skipped	No	36% (66)	65% (46)
	Yes	43% (42)	54% (56)

hoped to get a general indicator of perception of the school as threatening to the family as a unit. That is, status systems established by authorities may threaten not only one's self, but also those dear to him. Authorities are likely not to be respected if they are believed to cause the family to be uncomfortable.

Table 5 reports the proportion of students holding that *teachers* did not allocate status according to intellectual merit, that "you have to get in good with the teachers in order to get a fair grade." The data in Table 5 again show a sharp sex-difference, with boys again more alienated. A little over a quarter (26 per cent) of girls think teachers unfair, while 37 per cent of boys think so. Among the well behaved, however, the classroom status system administered by the teachers appears equally legitimate to boys and girls. The sex-difference is explained both by the greater number of rebels among boys, and by their greater alienation from the classroom status system.

Among girls rebellious classroom attitudes are apparently caused by flunking, but do not lead to rebellious behavior. The main relations in Table 5 are found between alienation from the classroom status system and classroom rebellion. Either flunking or being sent out of class is associated with high alienation, but skipping school is unrelated to thinking teachers unfair. Among those whose classroom behavior is rebellious, no further differences are associated with either receipt of flunk notices or skipping with a gang. Rebels, particularly classroom rebels, see their teachers as unfair.

Table 6 taps another type of officially administered status system, but with more diffuse standards of judgment. Coaches and other directors of student activities choose students for public performances, and also help determine students' status within the performing group. But judgments of athletic, musical, or dramatic "promise" are about as vague and unjustifiable as judgments of scholarly promise. Conse-

Table 6: Rebels more often say it is "certainly true" that coaches and supervisors of extra-curricular activities play favorites, among both girls and boys. Data for upper classmen.*

GIRLS

Receipt of Non-College Flunk Notice		Have *Not* Been Sent Out	Have Been Sent Out
		Per Cent Saying "Certainly True"	
Have **Not** Skipped	No	16% (293)	** (4)
	Yes	31% (42)	** (3)
Have Skipped	No	26% (81)	** (7)
	Yes	29% (31)	** (6)
	All who have been Sent Out		20% (20)

**Too few cases for meaningful percentages.

BOYS

Receipt of Non-College Flunk Notice		Have *Not* Been Sent Out	Have Been Sent Out
		Per Cent Saying "Certainly True"	
Have **Not** Skipped	No	24% (207)	30% (44)
	Yes	20% (60)	31% (29)
Have Skipped	No	47% (66)	50% (46)
	Yes	45% (42)	59% (56)

*In this case I have chosen the cutting point between "Certainly True" and other responses. This brings out more clearly both the sex-differences and the differences among types of rebels. The percentage answering "Probably True" runs in the opposite direction to the percentage answering "Certainly True." This would reduce the differences. But even using the less discriminating break leaves much of the difference intact. Among well-behaved boys, 53 per cent say the statement is either "certainly" or "probably" true; among the most extreme rebels, 70 per cent agree either positively or tentatively.

quently, we find that the extracurricular activities system as a whole is judged more harshly by students than the more restricted (or "functionally specific") system of classroom grading.

The kinds of rebels who hate coaches and supervisors most strongly are the truants, while those who hate teachers (see Table 5) are classroom rebels. It makes sense that alienation from the status system of the classroom, dealt with above, should be more closely related to classroom deviance (flunking and being sent out of class). Alienation from the "functionally diffuse" activities status system should be associated with "functionally diffuse" deviant behavior, like skipping school.

The officials of the school allocate not only desirable statuses. The rights of the status of "truant" are negligible, the duties onerous. The judgments that put people into such punishment statuses are generally (at least in English-speaking countries) based on more systematic collection of information than are favorable statuses. The concepts of "due process" ordinarily associated with such judging systems guarantee the "defendant" against certain kinds of information gathering, provide that the judge (or judges) shall be impartial, provide protection against certain methods of arrest and indictment which could punish before information was collected, and so forth.

Among such legal enforcement agencies, the school Attendance (or Principal's) Office has little formality. Further, there is in many cases a "presumption of guilt." When a teacher sends a student to the Attendance Office, he requires not a fair investigation of whose is the fault, but a support of his dramatic enforcement of classroom rules. Teachers demand that principals "back them up."[3]

We may expect, however, that the presumption of guilt

3. Cf. Howard S. Becker, "The Teacher in the Authority System of the Public School," *Journal of Educational Sociology*, Vol. 27 (November 1953), pp. 128-141, esp. pp. 133-139.

will fall most heavily on the rebels.[4] The association between rebellion and perception of the Attendance Office as unfair may partly reflect actual differences in experiences of fairness. But the fact remains that alienation from the legalistic Attendance Office is also part of the expressive alienation complex, as shown on Table 7.

Again boys are more alienated than girls. Twenty-two per cent of the boys, but only 12 per cent of the girls, agree that the Attendance Office is unfair. But the greater the degree of trouble with which the Attendance Office has dealt, the more students are likely to consider it unfair. Those who have been sent out of class, and those who combine skipping with having flunked, are particularly likely to consider the Attendance administration conspiratorial.

A final status system from which students can be alienated is the ranking of students among themselves. It is quite clear that prestige, responsibility, and privilege (e.g., at school functions) are differentially distributed among students, though no official administration of the student community creates the system. Status is allocated by diffuse criteria of "personality." Up to this point there has been a clear relation between the clarity and fairness of the standards applied and the perception of fairness. The Attendance Office, which operates on a more or less legal basis, was considered relatively legitimately run. Teachers, who have fairly clear intellectual standards for judging people, were perceived as less fair than the legalistic Attendance Office, but more fair than activities supervisors.

We would expect, on this basis, that the judgment of people in the informal student community would be perceived as unfair, because it, like the official student activities system, is "functionally diffuse." The standards by which status is awarded are not clear or in common agreement. The tabu-

4. Evidence on differential enforcement is presented in the Appendix on Method. Apparently the Attendance Office is more suspicious of known rebels.

Table 7: Rebels are more likely to see the Attendance Office as "out to get people," among both girls and boys. Data for upper classmen.

GIRLS

Receipt of
Non-College
Flunk Notice

		Have *Not* Been Sent Out	Have Been Sent Out
		Per Cent Seeing Unfairness	
Have **Not** Skipped	No	6% (293)	* (4)
	Yes	24% (42)	* (3)
Have Skipped	No	16% (81)	* (7)
	Yes	39% (31)	* (6)
		All who have been Sent Out	30% (20)

*Too few cases for meaningful percentages.

BOYS

Receipt of
Non-College
Flunk Notice

		Have *Not* Been Sent Out	Have Been Sent Out
		Per Cent Seeing Unfairness	
Have **Not** Skipped	No	16% (207)	21% (44)
	Yes	18% (60)	38% (29)
Have Skipped	No	17% (66)	30% (46)
	Yes	24% (42)	34% (56)

lation supports this expectation. A little over half consider that a small group of students "certainly" or "probably" run the activities (tabulation not presented here), and again rebels are more alienated than non-rebels (see Table 8).

A further interesting feature of this "activities" system is that the usual sex-differences in alienation do not appear; if anything they are reversed (choosing the breaking point between "Probably True" and "Probably False", 57 per cent of the girls give an alienated response, compared to 51 per cent of the boys).

We will consider sex-differences in more detail in following chapters; for the present we suggest that the marriage market and the community stratification system, on which girls' future status depends to a much greater extent than boys', are semi-legal or non-legal status systems. The ranking of persons in the student community by "personality" is also semi-legal; no one takes official responsibility for the rankings, and the standards are vague and erratic. To anticipate the analysis of following chapters, our interpretation of the sex-differences in alienation involves the following hypotheses:

(1) A boy's self-respect depends to a large extent on how highly his future in the labor market is evaluated, which is related in turn to school success. Consequently, the latter is more important to boys, and they react more strongly than girls to lack of success. They react to failure by interpreting the classroom and the other formal aspects of the school as unfair. But they also react by pretending the school has no importance to them at all, by being rebellious, by not working, although Chapter 6 will show that they have not given up desire for the rewards the school offers. Girls are much readier to give up the rewards which come with school success.

(2) A girl's future depends to a large extent on how favorably her personal qualities are evaluated by a future hus-

Table 8: Rebellious students, and girls, are more likely to say it is "Certainly True" that a small group runs student activities. Data for upper classmen.

GIRLS

Receipt of
Non-College
Flunk Notice

		Have *Not* Been Sent Out	Have Been Sent Out
		Per Cent Saying "Certainly True"	
Have **Not** Skipped	No	18% (293)	* (4)
	Yes	31% (42)	* (3)
Have Skipped	No	26% (81)	* (7)
	Yes	42% (31)	* (6)
	All who have been Sent Out		30% (20)

*Too few cases for meaningful percentages.

BOYS

Receipt of
Non-College
Flunk Notice

		Have *Not* Been Sent Out	Have Been Sent Out
		Per Cent Saying "Certainly True"	
Have **Not** Skipped	No	12% (207)	23% (44)
	Yes	18% (60)	28% (29)
Have Skipped	No	29% (66)	30% (46)
	Yes	26% (42)	38% (56)

band, but the systems for evaluating girls are, throughout their lives, diffuse and vague. In particular, success in the social swim in high school is a more important indication to a girl of how she is faring in the marriage market than is her success in school.

(3) Consequently, boys invest more of their self-respect in the formal system (grades, curriculum choices, college admissions) while girls invest more of their self-respect in the informal system.

(4) Status in the informal system, particularly for girls (who do not have *either* athletics *or* bright occupational futures as a claim to respect), is more dependent on family background than is status in the formal system.[5]

(5) These propositions imply certain relations between sex and alienation. First, girls should be more alienated from the informal system. We have already seen that boys are more alienated from the classroom status system administered by teachers, and from the Attendance Office. But we see from Table 5 that girls are more alienated from the student community than boys. The difference is too small to be reliable, but it suggests an opposite direction to previous sex-differences. As will be seen in Chapter 4, the reason that sex-differences with girls more alienated do not appear, is that participation in voluntary activities decreases alienation, and participation is also correlated with the importance of the system to one's self-respect (girls, for instance, participate more in student activities). Consequently, participation confounds the relation we are seeking here. When this confounding variable is removed, girls are much more alienated from the informal student community than boys.

These hypotheses anticipate the analysis of future chapters. They are raised here to call attention to the fact that the more conforming sex has more alienated attitudes toward

5.   This hypothesis will be used, along with the above hypotheses, to explain some results in Table 9 of this chapter.

the student community, even though *within* each sex the alienated attitudes are related to rebellion. This peculiar result *can* be explained by the hypotheses above; we hope to show later that it *ought* to be explained that way.

Aside from these provocative sex differences, the pattern of Table 8 supports the main hypothesis of this chapter: rebellious students are more likely to be alienated from the status system of the student community.[6]

The last status-alienation indicator is quite different in kind. If students feel that parents would be uncomfortable at school, or in school-connected functions, we may infer that students see the school as a status-threat to their families. The results of the tabulation of this question are presented in Table 9. The relation between rebellion and status threat to the family is not as strong as the relations in most of the tables in this chapter, but all except two of the comparisons between more rebellious and less rebellious students are in the right direction. More rebellious students are more alienated. There is one tie, and one inversion of only 2 per cent. (Both negative cases involve the lower right cell of boys.)

Again the sex-difference fails to appear: the relation between rebellion and perception of the school as a status-threat to the family seems to be stronger among girls. Further, we find a greater proportion of "Don't Know" responses among boys. These facts suggest that the status of the family of origin is more salient to girls than to boys. Boys, for whom family status may be less meaningful, bother less to make up their minds about how their parents might feel at school. Presumably they do not react to a perceived status-threat to the family by rebellious behavior as

6.   In Table 8, I have again chosen to use the break after "Certainly True," rather than the break between agreement and disagreement. The percentages for the extreme groups, using the weaker discrimination between agreement and disagreement, are 45 per cent alienated among the well-behaved boys and 59 per cent alienated among the worst-behaved boys. This is a sufficiently large difference to give confidence in stronger relations found using the better discrimination.

Table 9: Rebels are more likely to think most parents would feel uncomfortable around the school, among both girls and boys. Data for upper classmen.

GIRLS

Receipt of
Non-College
Flunk Notice

		Have *Not* Been Sent Out	Have Been Sent Out
		Per Cent Saying Parents Uncomfortable	
Have **Not** Skipped	No	36% (293)	* (4)
	Yes	52% (42)	* (3)
Have Skipped	No	47% (81)	* (7)
	Yes	55% (31)	* (6)
	All who have been Sent Out		70% (20)

*Too few cases for meaningful percentages.

BOYS

Receipt of
Non-College
Flunk Notice

		Have *Not* Been Sent Out	Have Been Sent Out
		Per Cent Saying Parents Uncomfortable	
Have **Not** Skipped	No	38% (207)	41% (44)
	Yes	42% (60)	45% (29)
Have Skipped	No	42% (66)	50% (46)
	Yes	48% (42)	48% (56)

much as girls do. Since the ranking of families, like the ranking of students by "personality," is functionally diffuse and semi-legal, this again suggests that girls tend to stake their self-conceptions more on the various "illegal" status systems, while boys organize their self-conception around the "legal" status systems.

In summary, rebellion, as indicated by truancy, difficulty in non-college courses, and by having been sent out of class, is related to alienation from various school status systems. Classroom rebellion is most closely related to perceptions of the classroom status system as unfair. Perception of the activities status system as unfair is related most closely to the diffuse offense of truancy. Multiple offenses, probably leading to a reputation as a "trouble-maker" and actual differential enforcement, lead to alienation from the legalistic Attendance Office status system. All kinds of rebellious behavior are related to alienation from the "informal" student status system. Rebellion among girls seems to be more strongly influenced by perception of the school as a threat to parental status; the relation between such perception and rebellion is quite weak among boys.

Further, it seems that the more diffuse the standards of the status system, the more likely it is to be perceived as unfairly administered. Activities officials and the student community are considered more unfair than are the teachers administering clearer standards of the classroom and the Attendance Office.

Finally, suggestive sex-differences in alienation were found. The more legal and functionally specific the standards and processes of a status system, the sharper were the sex-differences (with boys more alienated). The more diffuse the standards, the more likely girls were to be just as alienated as, or even more alienated than, boys. The more diffuse the standards, the more likely were sex-differences in the "Don't Know" rate, with boys answering "Don't Know" more often than girls in more diffuse systems, suggesting that these diffuse status systems involved the self-conception of boys to a lesser degree than the formal status systems, while for girls the opposite is true.

AUTONOMY, PERSONAL AND SOCIAL

A hedonistic attitude toward school, a negativistic attitude toward conformity among other adolescents, and alienation from both the school and the adolescent community are all characteristic of rebellious students. They define expressive alienation negatively and are attitudes about the moral worth of school. Rebels deny that school is worthwhile. But expressively alienated students not only deny the morality of the school; they also hold a positive morality of their own. The authoritative demands of the school are not only greeted with cynicism — they are greeted with moral indignation. The demand for autonomy from illegitimate adult interference is a positive moral claim against the school.

The autonomy of a clique or subculture in an organization does not become a salient problem, either to the institution or to the subgroup, unless the subgroup has a positive morality against the institution. For instance, if the internal morality of an autonomous group of workers supports high productivity, the effects are the same as if they had a positive attitude toward authority. Similarly the solidarity and autonomy of delinquents are salient to social workers, police, *and* to delinquents, precisely because their behavior will be different if they are autonomous. A subgroup with positive attitudes toward school and toward the law can have a high degree of internal solidarity and autonomy in decision making, without having to defend it. We need not assume that delinquent gangs have a higher degree of solidarity and autonomy than other cliques, but only that the solidarity is used in support of a deviant morality.

The solidarity of the delinquent gang is used, not only to protect offenders and ensure discipline in the commission of crimes, but also to claim certain rights vis-à-vis the adult community. That is, the rebellious peer group is oriented toward getting, from legitimate institutions, rights that the institutions are not enthusiastic about giving; the conforming peer group conversely helps the institutions enforce the obligations laid down by authoritative people. While the solidarity may be of equal quality, its structural implications are quite different.

The rights claimed by delinquent groups are suggested by an account of Hollingshead of an experiment with out-of-school youth. "If one tells him [a lower class boy] he is foolish to spend his money for old cars, flashy clothes, liquor, gambling, and sex one will be told forcibly — we experimented on this point with a few Class V's we knew well — 'No one can tell me how I am going to spend my money. Did you earn it?' This insistence upon freedom to do what he desires brings him into conflict with the law with significantly greater frequency than the other classes."[7]

The delinquent subculture, then, claims for adolescents the personal autonomy ordinarily associated with adulthood. Advice not to spend "his own money" on a car is as much an invasion of a boy's rights as such advice would be to adults. This claim of adult rights (and, less enthusiastically, adult duties) by people still subjected to the high school system of social control based on the doctrine of immaturity of adolescents creates severe conflicts. Even among teachers there is considerable disagreement about how far the school has the right to interfere with the non-academic life of students. But the school must assume, administratively, that its students are adolescents; some of the students, however, assume that they are adults.

The problem of the sources of adult claims will occupy us

7. A. B. Hollingshead, *Elmtown's Youth* (New York: John Wiley, 1949), p. 444.

Table 10: Rebels claim the right to smoke and oppose the
claims of the school to regulate, among both girls and boys.
Data for upper classmen.

GIRLS

Receipt of
Non-College
Flunk Notice

		Have Not Been Sent Out	Have Been Sent Out
		Per Cent Claiming Right to Smoke	
Have **Not** Skipped	No	6% (293)	* (4)
	Yes	26% (42)	* (3)
Have Skipped	No	17% (81)	* (7)
	Yes	45% (31)	* (6)
	All who have been Sent Out		30% (20)

*Too few cases for meaningful percentages.

BOYS

Receipt of
Non-College
Flunk Notice

		Have Not Been Sent Out	Have Been Sent Out
		Per Cent Claiming Right to Smoke	
Have **Not** Skipped	No	13% (207)	11% (44)
	Yes	17% (60)	31% (29)
Have Skipped	No	32% (66)	52% (46)
	Yes	40% (42)	59% (56)

Table 11: Rebels more often "Strongly Agree" that a car is necessary, among both girls and boys. Data for upper classmen.

GIRLS

Receipt of
Non-College
Flunk Notice

		Have *Not* Been Sent Out	Have Been Sent Out
		Per Cent "Strongly Agree"	
Have **Not** Skipped	No	5% (293)	* (4)
	Yes	10% (42)	* (3)
Have Skipped	No	12% (81)	* (7)
	Yes	35% (31)	* (6)
	All who have been Sent Out		20% (20)

*Too few cases for meaningful percentages.

BOYS

Receipt of
Non-College
Flunk Notice

		Have *Not* Been Sent Out	Have Been Sent Out
		Per Cent "Strongly Agree"	
Have **Not** Skipped	No	20% (207)	30% (44)
	Yes	25% (60)	28% (29)
Have Skipped	No	52% (66)	52% (46)
	Yes	50% (42)	62% (56)

in Chapter 5. For the present, we want to establish that such claims result in (or are caused by the same things that cause) rebellious behavior. For this purpose, we have asked students to agree or disagree with a claim of adult smoking and adult car-owning rights. The claim for rights to smoke is related to sex and rebellion in Table 10.

The strong and consistent relation (only one inversion; boys otherwise well behaved are not differentiated by having been kicked out of a class) supports the hypothesis strongly. Rebellious students object to the school's regulation of smoking, particularly off-campus. The claim to adult smoking rights characterizes rebels; the attribution of legitimacy to regulations enforcing adolescent status characterizes well-behaved students.

A similar question claiming that, like adults, adolescents can't get along without a car, shows a similarly strong relation. This is reported in Table 11.

As was the case with claims to smoking rights, boys are much more likely to claim adult rights than are girls. There are also marked differences between rebels and non-rebels. Among boys, the claim is particularly strongly related to truancy. If skipping indicates a generalized lack of commitment to the student role, this relation to truancy may be explained by noting that the generalized student role is an adolescent, age-graded role. An indicator of rebellion against the adolescent role is the claim to a "fair share" of the fun that comes with car ownership.

Adolescent rebels claim adult rights but also "cash in" those claims. Ownership of a car, as well as the conception that students have a right to a car, characterizes rebellious adolescents. Table 12 reports this behavioral claim to adult status, as related to rebellion. The behavioral and attitudinal patterns are almost the same, so a summary is superfluous.

Table 12: Rebels own more cars, among both girls and boys.
Data for upper classmen.

GIRLS

Receipt of
Non-College
Flunk Notice

		Have *Not* Been Sent Out	Have Been Sent Out
		Per Cent Owning Cars	
Have **Not** Skipped	No	6% (293)	* (4)
	Yes	5% (42)	* (3)
Have Skipped	No	10% (81)	* (7)
	Yes	23% (31)	* (6)
	All who have been Sent Out		15% (20)

*Too few cases for meaningful percentages.

BOYS

Receipt of
Non-College
Flunk Notice

		Have *Not* Been Sent Out	Have Been Sent Out
		Per Cent Owning Cars	
Have **Not** Skipped	No	29% (207)	36% (44)
	Yes	28% (60)	38% (29)
Have Skipped	No	53% (66)	41% (46)
	Yes	50% (42)	64% (56)

CONCLUSION

In this chapter we have been concerned not with the qualities of behavior, but with the qualities of persons who have engaged in certain kinds of behavior. By showing that rebellion is related to a series of attitudes, we have transformed the dependent variable of the study to an underlying psychological state named "expressive alienation." One of the manifest indicators of this underlying psychological state is the rebellious behavior we want to explain, although other behavior also reflects the underlying state. For instance, when put into a classroom where they do not rebel, expressively alienated students are more likely to be bored. Even when they do not skip school with a gang, students with this psychological state sometimes hate their conforming fellow students.

Our conception of the causal processes is not that students become bored with classes and then skip school (or vice versa). We rather suppose that students who become expressively alienated are more likely to be bored by any given class, and are more likely to be recruitable to any given gang of skipping kids. Even relatively unalienated students might have a run of bad luck with teachers and find half or more of their classes boring. Even alienated students might not have happened on a gang about to skip school.

One of the tests of the articulation hypothesis in Chapter 4, will be whether or not it explains expressive alienation that has not yet resulted in rebellion. On the other hand, some students who have committed rebellious acts are not very alienated — for instance, Table 1 shows that 41 per cent of the most rebellious boys do *not* have an emotional reaction of boredom with most of their classes. These relatively unalienated rebels may have been confronted with exceptional temptations, or they may have been alienated at one time and then, changed. If the theory of the causes of expressive alienation being developed here is valid, these unbored rebels ought to be more similar to non-rebels than to the bored rebels.

We hold, then, that some students are characterized by a complex of attitudes and behavior toward the school environment named "expressive alienation." Such alienated students are more likely than others to be rebellious — given the same opportunities, they are more likely to get into trouble. By establishing the correlation of rebellion to a number of other attitudes, we tentatively establish the emotional concomitants of this underlying state of alienation. The psychological state of expressive alienation, having as one of its manifestations rebellious *behavior,* has the following *attitudinal* manifestations:

(1) Short-run hedonism. Specifically, rebels tend to react by boredom in situations whose moral center is a long-run goal (classrooms), fail to see the connection between current deprivation (work) and long-run gratifications (grades), and give less importance to long-run gratifications.

(2) Negativism. Specifically, rebels reject people who conform ("squares").

(3) Alienation from the status systems either created by authorities or closely connected to legitimate institutions. This includes perception of the classroom, the Attendance Office, student activities, and the informal student community, as unfair. The rebel also more often perceives the institution of the school as a status threat to his parents.

(4) A culture of personal autonomy, holding that students have the same sort of rights as do adults, and specifically claiming adult car-owning and smoking rights.

The establishment of a complex concept made up of inherently connected elements gives us more theoretical hooks on which to hang an explanation of rebellion. An explanation of one of the elements should result in a partial explanation of the complex, including rebellion. And such a concept sets up standards of elegance in explanation, for the complete theory of rebellion must now explain not only rebellion itself but also the attitudes associated with rebellion.

From time to time results appeared, more or less incidentally in connection with the main purpose of this chapter, which suggested further lines of inquiry. The strong sex-differences in all but a few of the elements of expressive alienation (boys being more alienated) was one such result. The differential perception of status systems, according as the status system was more or less legalized, was another. And especially, the sex-differences themselves varied among the types of status system, with girls being more alienated from the highly diffuse systems.

The next two chapters (3 and 4) therefore turn to the relation between sex-roles, status systems, and expressive alienation. Chapter 5 will try to relate both sex-roles and status systems to the system of age-grading, since we have just shown that claims to adult status are part of expressive alienation. In Chapter 6 we will explore the relation between our findings and theories of psychological mechanisms producing deviant behavior.

3 The Labor Market and Rebellion: I

In this chapter we are laying the groundwork for a detailed test of the "articulation hypothesis": that high school rebellion, and expressive alienation, are most common among students who do not see themselves gaining an increment of future status from conformity in high school.

The first part of the argument is that this hypothesis is consistent with existing knowledge about the distribution of juvenile delinquency. Before arguing the hypothesis on the basis of data collected here, we want to make all possible use of previous knowledge. We will conclude, tentatively, that expressive alienation is concentrated among adolescents of school age, in that part of the adolescent population *who will make up* the manual working class in the next labor market cohort. Our presumption is that they perceive correctly their chances, and that this perception causes expressive alienation.

We will then examine in more detail the extant theory on conformity. First, we distinguish conformity in interpersonal relations and small groups, on the one hand, from conformity in public life on the other. Conformity in small groups depends mainly on the flow of gratifications and deprivations from other group members. Conformity in public life depends on so identifying oneself with a public role that future status in that role is important to self-respect, *and* on the extent to which future status is, indeed, allocated on criteria of conformity to the demands of the role.

The remainder of the chapter after the theoretical discussion attempts two goals. First, we try to show that boys destined for the manual working class show signs of poor articulation of present academic activity with future status. They are much less likely than either girls or boys marked for the upper middle class to express a clear curriculum interest. Since the curriculum or "track" is the main formal device connecting present activity with future status, this lack of curriculum interest indicates poor articulation.

We then examine the process by which girls avoid the problem of poor articulation; when girls come to believe that the good jobs allocated by the school are not for them, they substitute the role of housewife as an aspiration, with its attendant non-competitive standards. This preserves their self-respect even in the face of relative failure, which means that failure in school does not cut girls off from a public identity which can motivate conformity. As a direct check on this analysis of the meaning of being a girl and of the expectation of membership in the manual working class, we examine the responses of students on the importance of grades to securing good jobs. It appears that boys expecting low post-high school status do not see grades as of much importance to future success, indicating their perception of poor articulation.

In the course of this analysis, whose main object is to show poor perceived articulation is indeed most common in the categories that will comprise the manual work force, we locate other groups with poor articulation. Some girls have failed academically but have not reoriented to the marriage market, and they are caught in the same snare as boys who fail. And some girls have become so completely involved in futures as housewives that school has no vocational meaning at all. If the articulation hypothesis does explain the concentration of rebellion among boys who will be in the working class, then we must expect that the poor articulation of present activity with future status among these (relatively small) subgroups of girls will produce rebellion among them. This derived hypothesis is taken up in Chapter 4.

◆

"FACTS" OF DISTRIBUTION OF REBELLION

Since the attitudinal characteristics of high school rebels are similar to characteristics attributed to juvenile delinquents, we may make tentative inferences about rebellion from the facts of distribution of delinquency. The kind of juvenile delinquency of interest here involves *defiance* of the law and its official representatives. Multiple offenses, lack of care in avoiding police and school authorities, refusing to use social skills to influence police and courts, should be more characteristic of expressively alienated delinquents than of juveniles who merely evade the law; and all these patterns of behavior should increase the likelihood of a delinquency showing up in official rates. Consequently, the distribution of official delinquency in the society is a more illuminating fact for our discussion than would be the distribution of "real" delinquency.

Albert K. Cohen summarizes the evidence of official statistics as follows: "It is our conclusion, by no means novel or startling, that juvenile delinquency and the delinquent subculture in particular are overwhelmingly concentrated in the male, working-class sector of the juvenile population."[1] And later: "It does not follow, however, that the popular

---

1. *Delinquent Boys, op. cit.*, p. 37.

impression that juvenile delinquency *is primarily a product of working-class families and neighborhoods is an illusion.*"[2]

This statement of the "facts" of distribution is, I think, inadequate, for the implicit hypothesis in the underscored phrase is not sufficient to explain the material on delinquency distribution.

In the first place, if delinquency is a "product" of working class socialization, the sex-differences remain unexplained. Though little is known about it, it does not appear likely that the socialization of working class girls *in the family and neighborhood* is much different from the socialization of boys. The marked differentiation of treatment of children according to sex seems not to occur until the pre-adolescent period, when much of the life of the child is lived in the peer group and the school.

Second, this hypothesis (or "fact" of distribution) does not account for the rather marked ethnic differences in official delinquency. Almost all the depressed ethnic groups (Negroes, Spanish-Americans, Italians a generation or two ago) have considerably higher delinquency rates than Protestant whites of the same class background. Though investigation here is also inadequate, there is no proven commonality in the socialization of *different* urban depressed minorities that can explain this fact.

We have to find a formulation of the "facts" of distribution that economically organizes at the same time ethnic, social class, ecological, and sex differences in official delinquency rates. It is our contention that the formulation that can do this refers to the *future* status of the adolescent, rather than to the status of his family of origin. Girls differ markedly from boys not so much by previous socialization as by the status they can ordinarily expect to achieve as housewives whose position depends on the husband's occupation, rather than as workers whose status depends on their own qualifications. The common element differentiating de-

2. *Ibid.,* p. 42, my emphasis.

pressed ethnic groups from other working class populations is their *public* status in the labor market, their occupational life-chances, rather than their patterns of early socialization.[3] It is well-known from studies of social mobility that working class children are less likely to succeed in the occupational world than middle class children;[4] that is, girls, majority ethnic groups, middle class children, all more rarely end up as workers, and all rarely become juvenile delinquents.

But some working class children do move up occupationally, and some middle class children fall below their parents' status. If we organize our discussion of the "facts" of distribution around the future status of adolescents, the fact of social mobility becomes potentially important in accounting for middle class delinquency and working class conformity.

Finally, given a certain level of origin, the community context greatly influences the future of adolescents. In Berkeley, California, for instance, a very large proportion of Negroes and working class children go on to college.[5] In many slum areas, on the other hand, principals can number the college entrants for the last five or ten years on the fingers of one hand.[6]

In other words, the reformulated "facts" of distribution of official delinquency are that it is concentrated in those sectors of the adolescent population *who will make up* the manual working class in the next labor market cohort (males, of working class origin, especially in depressed ethnic groups, and especially in slum areas where schools provide

3.   The point that racial and ethnic prejudice is primarily a pattern of institutionalizing public life, rather than a matter of interpersonal relations, is made by Herbert Blumer, "Race Prejudice as a Sense of Group Position," *Pacific Sociological Review,* Vol. 1 (Spring 1958), pp. 3-7.
4.   For a summary, see Seymour M. Lipset and Reinhard Bendix, *Social Mobility in Industrial Society* (Berkeley: University of California Press, 1959), *passim.*
5.   An unpublished study by Lloyd Street.
6.   A striking instance of this influence of community context on labor market processes is described in Norman Dennis, *et al., Coal is Our Life* (London: Eyre and Spottiswoode, 1956), pp. 176-178.

few students with the chance to move up). The causal chain
might take either direction. Rebelliousness of Negroes might
be the cause of their likelihood of becoming manual workers.
And the conformity of girls might keep them out of the working class. We will try to show that the main causal process
is that of an undesirable future producing adolescent rebellion.

With this key "fact" for guidance, we go on to discuss certain other "facts" of distribution of juvenile delinquency: its
distribution among the age-grades, its urban-rural distribution, and its (relatively uninvestigated) distribution among
societies.

It is silly, of course, to discuss the distribution of "juvenile
delinquency" among the age-grades; its place in the age-
grading system is part of its definition. But a discussion of
the distribution of "expressive alienation," which is not inherently an age-graded concept, is valid among the age-
grades. The evidence is rather scanty, but certain clues do
exist.

Much of the public life of adults is in their occupations.
Therefore, investigations of indiscipline in the work place,
of dissatisfaction with work, of alienation from the status
systems of the work place, bear indirectly on the problem of
how much expressive alienation is found among the adult
population.

The short-run hedonistic orientation of manual workers
is described by Richard Hoggart,[7] in implicit contrast to the
long-run orientation of the middle class. Since work itself
has the most long-run orientation of most people's activities,
it is significant that manual workers are considerably less satisfied with their work than are middle class people.[8] But the
largest share of even manual workers report that they are

7. *The Uses of Literacy* (London: Chatto and Windus, 1957), pp.
110-123.
8. Cf. Robert Blauner, "Attitudes Toward Work: A Discussion of Research," in Walter Galenson and S. M. Lipset, eds., *Labor and Trade
Unionism* (New York: John Wiley, 1960), pp. 341-345.

satisfied with their work.[9] If we can take enjoyment of work as an indicator of a more long-run orientation, manual workers evidently have more of a short-run hedonistic orientation than do middle class people.[10] But it is doubtful if hedonism is as prevalent among workers as it is among high school rebels, for most do like their work.

Though indiscipline, lack of responsiveness to legitimate orders and rules, is certainly common in work life (especially, again, among manual workers), the literature implies that the degree of indiscipline is not so great as to make it consistently problematic whether order will be maintained. But order is problematic in schools. "Indiscipline" as a mass phenomenon in the work place tends not to be open defiance as in schools (at least in America), but "systematic withdrawal of efficiency." The evasion of production standards, not rebellion of flouting of the rules, is the common form of worker alienation.

The syndrome of alienation from the status system among (particularly manual) workers is described by Peter Drucker: "From the point of view of the worker . . . selection for promotion is irrational and bewilderingly haphazard. It seems to be based on nothing but the arbitrary whims of a

9.   *Ibid.*, pp. 340-341.
10.   Indirect evidence on the short-run hedonistic attitude of manual workers is available from several kinds of studies. Some evidence, for example, indicates that workers (and more especially workers' children) tend to perceive the relevance of objects to short-run activity, and to see only the consequences of action in the immediate future. They do not consistently think of objects and acts in a frame of reference of an extended time-span. See B. Bernstein, "Some Sociological Determinants of Perception," *British Journal of Sociology*, Vol. 9 (June 1958), pp. 159-174. Some of the work on deferred gratification patterns is also relevant. For instance, Leonard Reissman, "Levels of Aspiration and Social Class," *American Sociological Review*, Vol. 18 (June 1953), pp. 233-242, and Louis Schneider and Sverre Lysgaard, "The Deferred Gratification Pattern: A Preliminary Study," *American Sociological Review*, Vol. 18 (April 1953), pp. 142-149. We argue for a somewhat different interpretation of some of these materials in Chapter 5. Quite often people oriented toward the middle class do not defer gratification so much as claims to adult rights. Students oriented to the middle class may find it immediately gratifying to be adolescent.

management quite remote and personally almost unknown to the men in the ranks."[1]

Though it is hazardous to make a judgment in the absence of systematic evidence, it seems that "expressive alienation" does often characterize manual workers who tend to be hedonistic, to reject authority, to be alienated from the status system. But manual workers do not seem to be as alienated as adolescents *who are going to become* manual workers. Relatively rarely does adult delinquency take on the vandalistic, authority-fighting quality of adolescent delinquency. Official adult delinquency tends to be an occupation, and confined to a few, rather than an expression of alienation.[2]

Next, it is quite well established that official juvenile delinquency is considerably more common in large cities than in rural areas, though this difference is apparently decreasing. Juvenile delinquency seems to be more prevalent in modern industrial society than it was in the agricultural past, or than it is now in primitive societies. The evidence on this point is quite weak; rather than documenting inadequate evidence, we will use the tentative fact for suggestive purposes.

There appears to be a concentration of expressive alienation in the in-school age groups where adolescents have to face finding a job in a labor market that uses "fair" standards rather than family influence in the distribution of good jobs. Metropolitan labor markets are more universalistic or fair than rural ones; labor markets in industrial societies more universalistic than in agricultural ones.[3] When schools come

1. *Concept of the Corporation* (New York: John Day, 1946), pp. 144-145.
2. Edwin H. Sutherland, *The Professional Thief* (Chicago: University of Chicago Press, 1937).
3. It has been suggested that age-grading itself only becomes important in universalistic societies. See S. N. Eisenstadt, *From Generation to Generation* (Glencoe: The Free Press, 1956). By "universalism" we mean that acquiring a good job depends more on what you know than on who your father was.

to influence the distribution of good jobs in a society, the in-school age-grades tend to develop expressively alienated sub-groups.[4]

If future research should not overturn the more speculative of the "facts" of distribution of delinquency (and implicitly, of expressive alienation), we may state the following general "fact" of distribution: Expressive alienation appears to be most common among *the adolescents of school age* who are exposed to *more universalistic labor markets*, and who *will fill* the manual working class positions in those markets.

We do not have several of the relevant variables to work with here. We have only adolescents, only in one community context in a universalistic-achievement society. We have no significant ethnic minority. We will therefore have to confine our internal analysis to sex, social class, and school achievement as independent variables, orientation to the labor market and to age-grading systems as intervening variables, and expressive alienation as a dependent variable.

Before beginning the analysis proper, it will be convenient to summarize the extant theory on conformity in public life, particularly in organizations. This theory has been somewhat confused by the notion that current behavior is governed by the past (socialization), and part of it has been confused by the notion that formal organizations are unimportant to personalities, that conformity must "really" depend on interpersonal relations. With very slight restatement and selection, however, the theory of organizational conformity is serviceable for our purposes.

---

4.   Of the in-school age-grades, those who have quit school are probably the most alienated, because they are the most likely to become members of the working class. Also, alienation is apt to result in either quitting or expulsion.

THE CONTINGENCY OF FUTURE STATUS
ON CURRENT PERFORMANCE

Life in organizations of public life, such as the school, the factory, the army, is embedded in multiple status systems. People make judgments of the relative worth of others according to many standards, from different (official and unofficial) strategic places in the flow of rewards. Judgments of intelligence and achievement, of efficiency and profitability, of honor and dishonor, permeate public life. In the family or intimate friendship group, personal worth is not supposed to govern the allocation of rewards, or at least to govern it to a lesser extent. In intimate primary groups, status and reward are supposed to depend on need, rather than ability.

Conformity in families and friendship groups, then, depends on personal commitments to relatives and friends; conformity in public life depends on commitments to a conception of oneself that will be damaged by unfavorable judgments by people in authority. To become dishonored in an army means that the rights, duties, and respect from significant others which have heretofore been associated with the soldier's conception of his future will no longer be available. Discharge for incompetence means, to a craftsman, that he cannot command the labor market rights or perform the labor market duties he had associated with his career plans. (This is besides the immediate punishment of loss of pay.)

Conformity in public life, then, rarely depends either on interpersonal commitments or on the constant maintenance of a favorable gratification-deprivation balance, motivating people from one moment to the next. It rather depends on people holding a relatively vivid image of a future desirable status if they conform now, and of a punishing status if they withdraw efficiency, or panic in the face of enemy fire, or do poorer school work than they might. If an organization can offer career rewards for conformity, its discipline tends to be high. If the careers are not attractive, or not dependent on present performance, discipline tends to be low.[5]

Among organizations perhaps none depends more on a future orientation than the schools, especially secondary schools and higher education. In a fair and competitive labor market (or in modern techniques of winning husbands through dating), adult status is less determined by characteristics of the family of origin than by performance in the public, age-graded school system. If the school is well articulated with the labor market so that current performance is known by students to affect future status in a specifiable way, then conformity tends to be high — and the higher the post-educational status appears to the individual, the greater will be his motivation to conform.[6]

The high school, then, is assigned its population on the

5. The most extensive discussion is Weber's, especially in his treatment of bureaucracy. The divorce of organizational status allocation from influence of families, career commitment of the bureacrat to the organization, and continuous exercise of the rights and duties of the status, underlie bureaucratically rational disciple. See in his *From Max Weber: Essays in Sociology* (New York: Oxford University Press, 1946), pp. 196-197 and 202-204. For some of the considerations brought up by non-bureaucratic administration, see my "Bureaucratic and Craft Administration of Production," *Administrative Science Quarterly*, Vol. 4 (September 1959), pp. 168-187, and "Some Social Supports of Professional Attitudes among Construction Workers," presented at meetings of the American Sociological Society, September 1959. Of course, by emphasizing career commitment I do not mean to deny other causes of conformity. Day-to-day gratifications, in the form of pay, are crucial to conformity in factories. Coercion, loyalty to friends, and ideological commitment play a crucial role in conformity in armies. Traditional respect for lords and kings forms the core of conformity in patrimonial administration. I emphasize careers here because they are at the center of problems of school authority.

6. For instance, it seems that children of workers who come to universities and colleges absorb *more* rapidly and completely the formal and informal values represented by the faculty than do middle class children. It will be noted that this relation is the reverse of that holding in high schools. The reason seems to be that workers' children in college become middle class, a higher status to them than to middle class children.

unachieved basis of age. It allocates the futures it has to offer on the basis of achieved academic performance, placing the ascriptively assigned non-achievers into a condition of strain, in which present performance does not seem to be rewarded by status increment in the future.

◆

SEX DIFFERENCES IN THE
MEANING OF FAILURE

Before a status system can operate for conformity, it must be salient to the people involved. And conversely, the more important a status system is to the self-conception of a person, the more punishing will be his failure. If it is assumed that one reaction to punishment in a status system is rebellion, we derive the paradoxical result that non-conformity increases as the forces working to make conformity important increase.[7]

The alienative effect of a status system, working through a threat to self-respect, *may* be dealt with by substituting another scale of personal worth for the threatening one. But this will be more or less possible according as there are or are not other status systems defined as legitimate refuges. The sex-division of labor in the society, with a large proportion of women being occupied in keeping house for a major share of their lives, provides to girls an alternative system of self-judgment to the labor market. Boys, on the other hand, are required to judge themselves according to "what they will amount to" in the labor market.

We may use as an indicator of orientation to becoming a housewife the answers of girls to the two questions: "What type of job would you like most of all to be doing ten years from now?" and "What sort of job do you think you will probably *really have* ten years from now?" If girls gave "housewife" as an answer to either or both of these questions,

7.   This paradoxical argument will form the center of Chapter 6.

they will be considered oriented to marriage. Those girls who checked occupations as answers to both questions may be considered most oriented to the labor market. Other answers (involving "Don't Know") will be considered ambiguous.

First, we may contrast the level of aspiration and expectation of boys with girls who chose labor market occupations on both questions. This is done in Table 13. Two points of immediate value may be seen from the table above. First, girls are, obviously, oriented to the labor market only in its upper reaches, 87 per cent desiring either professional or lower middle class jobs. Among boys, only 41 per cent are so oriented.

Table 13:   Nearly all girls who want and expect to be work-ing in ten years expect white collar jobs, while many boys expect to be manual workers. Boys have much more conflict between levels of aspiration and levels they expect to reach.

Aspirations and Expectations	Girls	Boys
Upper Middle Class[a] on Both	47%	29%
Lower Middle Class on Both[b]	40%	12%
Skilled and Farm Manual on Both	3%	21%
Unskilled on Both	–	12%
Aspirations Higher than Expectations	9%	22%
Expectations Higher than Aspirations	0%[c]	5%
Total	99%	101%
Number	233	581

a. Professionals and a very few entertainers and airline steward-esses.

b. Clerical, Sales, and Small Business aspirations and expecta-tions.

c. Less than 0.5%.

Further, the entries labeled "Aspirations Higher than Expectations" and "Expectations Higher than Aspirations" indicate the lack of escape for boys, if they aspire to jobs they don't think they can acquire. A total of 27 per cent of boys, but only 9 per cent of girls, are put into this situation of conflict. The same type of conflict is probably represented by the various ambiguous answers, not included in the table. Of 748 boys, 167 (22 per cent) gave a "Don't Know" response to one of the questions on their future; only 51 of the 668 girls (7 per cent) gave ambiguous answers.

The hypothesis suggested by the above data is that girls, when confronted with the problem of not being able to reach high aspirations, tend to substitute standards of housewifely success as a system of self-evaluation. We will show first that lack of success in school causes girls to reorient to marriage. Boys, of course, cannot reorient, so they must face lack of success in the only post-high school status system available to them. We will then present evidence that the substitution of marriage aspirations by girls, to protect their self-respect, explains the sex-difference in expressive alienation.

SCHOOL STATUS AND STATUS SYSTEM SUBSTITUTION

Our object in this section is to demonstrate a tendency for girls who are low in school achievement to form an image of their future in marriage rather than in the labor market. Accordingly, we will compare girls oriented to the labor market with those partly or fully committed to marriage. If the substitution of status systems works according to the hypothesis, girls oriented to the labor market should be more successful in school, on the average, than girls partly oriented to marriage, and both should be more successful than girls fully oriented to marriage.

As indices of school success we may use the proportion of students reporting that they have a "B" average or better, the proportion in the high ability classes in English, the proportion reporting that they have never received a flunk notice, and the proportion having taken algebra as their freshman mathematics class. The results of the relevant tabulations are presented in Table 14.

Table 14:   School achievement of girls oriented to the labor market is higher than that of girls oriented to marriage.*

Girls Oriented To:	Percentage with B's or Better	Percentage in High Abil. Eng.	Percentage Never Flunked	Percentage Who Took Albegra	N
Labor Market	47%	42%	79%	36%	233
Both Marriage and Labor Market	35%	38%	78%	32%	231
Marriage	27%	29%	65%	24%	153
Ambiguous	22%	31%	65%	41%	51

*Girls who gave an occupation as both aspiration and expectation were classified as oriented to the labor market. If there was at least one occupational answer and at least one "housewife" answer, they were classified as oriented to both. If there were only housewife answers, they were considered fully committed to the marriage market. Others (those having at least one "Don't Know" or at least one "No Answer") were classified as "Ambiguous."

Though the differences are quite small in some cases, it is clear that orientation to the labor market is associated with high achievement, and orientation to the marriage market with low achievement. All the differences are in the expected direction, tentatively establishing that low status girls do substitute a housewife image of their future if they are unsuccessful in school.

The "ambiguous" image may be better understood by considering the above table. As with girls oriented to the labor market, girls giving "Don't Know" answers were more likely than others to have taken algebra during their freshman year. But like the girls oriented to the marriage market, they have low achievement in school, receiving more flunk notices, earning lower grade averages, and standing in the lower ability groups in English. We may surmise that these girls have been oriented to the labor market, have failed to achieve, but have not substituted the marriage market as a system of self-evaluation.

THE SEX DIVISION AND ARTICULATION OF THE FUTURE WITH THE PRESENT

Before the material on the sex division and rebellion can be properly interpreted, it is necessary to deal with the differential effectiveness of the mechanisms connecting images of the future to current activity. In the formal system of the high school, these mechanisms are the *curricula* or "tracks." The curricula are supposed to contain the culture on the basis of which future status is awarded. If students perceive that the course content does not appreciably affect their future, current work does not "make sense."

Because girls oriented to the labor market (or better, nearly all girls to the extent they are oriented to the labor market) are seeking the clerical and professional sectors, their future status is determined by school performance. Boys oriented to the lower middle class rarely aim to be clerks; they aim for the small business sector, and this is the main part of the middle class where status is not allocated on the basis of education. Manual work, also, is seldom allocated on the basis of education.

If we classify the sexes into those oriented to (1) the professional sector of the labor market, (2) all other sectors of the labor market, (3) both marriage and labor markets, and (4) fully to marriage, we can compare the pattern of curriculum interest among the comparable subgroups of boys and girls. That is, boys and labor-market oriented girls will appear in categories (1) and (2); the rest of the girls, who have images inapplicable to boys, will appear in (3) and (4).

Contrasts in the curriculum interest between the sexes in the first two categories will give a notion of the sex-differences in the articulation of school with images of the future. Image of the future is related to curriculum interest in Table 15.

It is clear from Table 15 that the pattern of curriculum interest among potentials for elite positions is roughly similar between the sexes. Almost all are on college preparatory curricula. But among those oriented to the labor market in positions *below* those of the professionals, 66 per cent of the girls and only 30 per cent of the boys are "most interested" in vocational curricula presumably leading to those positions. It might be thought that this could be explained entirely by the remaining differences in the class level of the positions aimed for and expected by boys and girls. But if, as seen in Table 16, we take only the boys and girls aspiring to enter the lower middle class, the difference remains.

Almost four out of five (79 per cent) of the girls whose job aspirations are lower middle class, but less than half (43 per cent) of the boys, are on vocational curricula. Further, almost all the girls are on the "Business Education" curriculum, while many of the boys who do choose vocational curricula choose "Industrial Arts," preparatory to working class positions.

Of course, the key to this difference in curriculum choice is the different distribution of lower middle class positions aspired to. We find that 82 per cent of the lower middle class male answers are for small business aspirations, 13 per cent for sales, and 6 per cent for clerical work. Only 10 per

Table 15:   Girls with lower aspirations choose vocational
curricula more often than boys with lower aspirations. Percentage choosing various curricula.

Curriculum Interest[a]

Image of Future and Sex	College Prepar- atory	Voca- tional	Ambig- uous	Total
Labor Market Oriented				
Upper Middle Class, Girls[b]	82%	8%	10%	100% (122)
Upper Middle Class, Boys[b]	77%	14%	10%	101% (198)
Lower than Upper Middle, Girls[c]	15%	66%	18%	99% (163)
Lower than Upper Middle, Boys[c]	17%	30%	54%	101% (553)
Marriage Oriented				
Both Occupation and Housewife	31%	47%	21%	99% (213)
Housewife on Both	18%	41%	42%	101% (160)

a. "Vocational" includes industrial arts, vocational agriculture,
    and business education. "Ambiguous" includes general educa-
    tion, don't know, and no answer.

b. Those who answered professional, entertainer, or airline
    stewardess on both aspirations and expectations, or one of
    these on aspiration and "Don't Know," or no answer on expec-
    tations, were classified as having upper middle class orienta-
    tions.

c. "Lower than Upper Middle" includes all responses which in-
    cluded lower occupations than those above (e.g., professional
    aspirations but unskilled expectations would be here). Many of
    the girls answered clerical and secretarial work to both ques-
    tions. If either of the answers was housewife, they were put
    into a marriage market group.

cent of the girls' aspirations are for small business, only 8
per cent for sales, and 82 per cent for clerical work.[8] The
bureaucratic occupations of clerical work are allocated on

8.   Tabulations not presented separately here.

Table 16:   Girls aspiring to the lower middle class often choose vocational curricula; boys aspiring to the same class level more seldom choose vocational curricula. Percentage choosing various curricula.

| | Curriculum Interest | | | |
Aspirations and Sex	College Prepar= atory	Voca- tional	Ambig- uous	Number
Girls Aspiring to Lower Middle Class*	8%	79%	13%	223
Boys Aspiring to Lower Middle Class	19%	43%	38%	126

*"In a small business for yourself," "Clerical or secretarial work," or "Sales clerk or salesman."

the basis of education; the petty bourgeois positions are not.[9]

To show that the ambiguous answers on the curriculum question do reflect a perception of poor articulation between the future and the present, we may consider the answers to the question: "How important would you say your grades were to getting the kind of job you want?" The proportion of students saying grades are "Very Important" is an indicator of the concrete meaning of curricula and aspirations, of how the quality of the connection between school and life is transmitted to students' evaluations of rewards in the classroom. The distribution of answers to this question for students oriented to different sections of the labor market and to marriage, and interested in different curricula, is presented in Table 17.

The boys and girls oriented to the professional sector of the labor market, as expected, consider grades very important to getting good jobs. But girls oriented to lower posi-

9. See the evidence summarized in S. M. Lipset and R. Bendix, *Social Mobility* . . . , *op. cit.*, pp. 171-180.

tions also tend to consider grades very important to labor market success; boys are less likely to consider them important. Students giving ambiguous answers to the curriculum question, and boys giving vocational answers, see less connection between current performance and future status.

In addition to the comparisons between labor market oriented girls and boys, we may consider the situation of girls oriented to marriage. Earlier (see Table 15) we found that nearly half of the girls fully committed to marriage gave ambiguous answers on the curriculum question. This suggests that they, like many boys, are put in a situation in which future status is not contingent on current performance. This

Table 17:   Percentage considering grades "very important" to getting good jobs, by sex, labor market orientations*, and curriculum interest.

	Curriculum Interest		
Sex and Image of Future	College Preparatory	Vocational	Ambiguous
Labor Market			
Upper Middle Class, **Girls**	74% (100)	50% (10)	50% (12)
Upper Middle Class, **Boys**	68% (151)	52% (27)	80% (20)
Lower than Upper Middle, **Girls**	84% (25)	56% (108)	47% (30)
Lower than Upper Middle, **Boys**	59% (93)	48% (163)	37% (297)
Marriage Market			
Both Occupation and Housewife	60% (70)	57% (106)	53% (47)
Housewife on Both	50% (28)	52% (65)	34% (67)

*See notes to Table 15 above for classification according to labor market orientation.

suggestion is further supported by the data in Table 17. Girls fully oriented to marriage are less likely than any other group of girls to consider grades important for getting good jobs. In two out of three cases, in fact, they are less likely to consider them important than are boys oriented to lower positions in the labor market. The girls fully committed to marriage, whose curriculum interest indicates the poorest connection between current performance and future status (giving ambiguous answers), give less importance to grades than any other cell in the table (34 per cent).

In other words, some girls have so completely substituted a housewife image for the labor market that their high school experience is no longer meaningful, even in a transitional labor market sense. High school courses are not connected, in a valid fashion, with their images of the future. This creates some problems for the analysis. For if we are to support the hypothesis that being bound to the labor market creates special problems for the unsuccessful, we would have to compare lower achieving girls who remain oriented to the labor market with girls oriented to marriage. We would have to show that those to whom the substitution of status systems is not available (for reasons explored in Chapter 5) are more rebellious. But the hypothesis of this section gives opposite results. According to the hypothesis of articulation, future housewives, especially those not indicating interest in any curricula, should be most rebellious. However we try to escape this problem, it is bound to be intricate: these complexities will be dealt with in the next chapter.

THE HYPOTHESIS OF ARTICULATION
RESTATED

We suggest that the key to high school rebellion is to be found in the status prospects of students, rather than in their status origins. Juvenile delinquency statistics can be organized by the idea that expressive alienation is concentrated in adolescent populations confronted with a future of manual labor in a universalistic labor market. This suggests that the key fact is the future of students, not their origins. Since we know that origins partly determine futures, social class will be an important variable, but in an unusual way.

In order to secure conformity from students, the high school must articulate academic work with careers of students, although the careers are in the labor market and in households, outside the school. Various subgroups of students, holding different positions with respect to these external structures, create problems of authority within the high school.

First, girls who think they are going into the labor market almost unanimously aim for positions in the upper middle class or the bureaucratic sector of the lower middle class. If they are not oriented to these labor market sectors, they are oriented to marriage. Boys, on the other hand, are trapped by the labor market. They cannot get out of it, even when they face an "unsuccessful" future in it; one indication of the dilemma is that boys are much more likely to aspire to jobs they do not expect to get than are girls.

This poorer articulation of academic work with imagined future careers is reflected in boys' ambiguous answers to the curriculum interest question. Curriculum choice is a behavioral index of perceived articulation, for it is the formal device of articulation. A question asking students directly how much academic success matters in the labor market supports this interpretation: boys, especially boys giving vocational and ambiguous answers on the curriculum question and aiming for lower labor market positions, are much less likely to say that grades are important in getting good jobs. Since curriculum interest functions well to measure perceived articulation, and since it is a behavioral variable with meaning in real life rather than merely an attitude question, we will use it as an indicator of articulation in the following argument.

We have located two small subgroups of girls who are similar to boys in articulation of the present and future. First, a few girls remain oriented to the labor market in the face of failure. They are precisely similar to boys in the sources of poor articulation. Second, girls completely oriented to the marriage market are also aiming for statuses they do not hope to reach by academic achievement. These small subgroups of girls will form the basis for the first main argument for the theory of articulation in the next chapter. The task of the next chapter is to show that those groups of students with the poorest articulation between current academic activity and future status increment are most expressively alienated.

The chain of causes we propose to explain the distribution of expressive alienation, then, takes roughly the following form:

(1) Students' chances of success in the post-high school job market are determined by origin, ability, school attended, sex, and so forth.

(2) The perceived value of school depends on the school's perceived connection with success. This perceived connection varies among social classes, ability groups, sexes, races, and neighborhoods.

(3) Perceived lack of connection of school work to occupational success produces rebellion.

(4) Perception is roughly accurate on these questions, hence rebellion is concentrated in groups which actually have poor articulation of current work with future status.

4 The Labor Market and Rebellion: II

Our argument for the hypothesis of the previous chapter is indirect. So far we have been trying to show that the hypothesis is sufficient to explain the well-known fact that rebellion is concentrated among less intelligent boys, to whom current academic activity does not have a clear connection to future status increment. If poor articulation does explain their greater rebellion, then we can derive other consequences from the hypothesis of articulation which will serve to support it.

First, we will analyze rates of rebellious behavior in an attempt to show that the small groups of girls who have poor articulation are similar to boys in their degree of alienation. If we are successful in locating rebellious girls by the theory, the theory is shown to be better than the common sense generalization about less intelligent boys.

Second, we will consider the evidence on a main alternative theory, that social class origin explains the distribution of rebellion. The presentation of evidence discrediting this alternative will strengthen our argument.

Finally, we will try to show that the theory helps interpret the relation between rebellion and expressive alienation. Specifically, we will show that those students who are alienated from the school *but* who have not actively rebelled are as likely to have poor articulation as the rebels. Conversely, we will demonstrate that those students who have rebelled but who do not (at least not now) hold rebellious attitudes, have good articulation. That is, we will show that the theory predicts the underlying psychological attribute of expressive alienation, whether or not this alienation happens to have resulted in rebellious behavior.

If the theory withstands these three indirect tests, we can place more confidence in its capacity to explain the facts which originally suggested it, then go on to examine the cultural and psychological processes that create this structural relation.

◆

REBELLION AND ORIENTATION TO THE FUTURE

Table 18 presents the proportion of students who have either skipped school or been sent out of class or both, according to orientation to the future, curriculum interest, and sex. These three variables combined produce an ordering of students according to articulation of the present with the future.

In any sex and orientation group, those giving ambiguous answers to the curriculum question can be assumed to have poorer articulation. In any one curriculum group, those aiming for and expecting to achieve higher statuses can be assumed to have better articulation, and to see current academic activity as meaningful. Since girls on vocational curricula are destined for the bureaucratic labor market, while boys on such curricula will join the working class labor market, girls on vocational curricula should have much better articulation than boys. Consequently we expect to find the

Table 18: Percentage who have skipped or been sent out, by sex, image of the future, and curriculum interest.

| | Curriculum Interest | | |
Image of the Future and Sex	College Preparatory	Vocational	Ambiguous
Labor Market Oriented			
Upper Middle, **Girls**	9% (100)	10% (10)	17% (12)
Upper Middle, **Boys**	29% (151)	41% (27)	30% (20)
Lower than Upper Middle, Girls	28% (25)	23% (108)	23% (30)
Lower than Upper Middle, Boys	32% (93)	47% (163)	55% (297)
Marriage Oriented			
Partly Committed to Marriage Market	17% (70)	27% (106)	30% (47)
Fully Committed to Marriage Market	25% (28)	26% (65)	39% (67)

largest sex-difference in rebellion among those with vocational curriculum interests. Girls fully committed to marriage without any curriculum interest were shown to have very poor articulation, and consequently should be among the most rebellious girls, according to the theory.

On the basis of the analysis above, we expect the following patterns to appear in the table:

(1) Among those oriented to a particular level in the labor market or to the marriage market, those giving ambiguous answers to the curriculum question should be more rebellious. In four of the six lines, the figure on the right is greater than others on the same line, which bears out the hypothesis. Of the two failures, one is not very serious. Those boys who

aim for the upper middle class but who are *on curricula aimed for the working class* (answering "vocational") are more rebellious. Their career bewilderment is probably nearly as great as that of boys headed for the upper middle class who answer "Don't Know" to the curriculum question. Consequently this inversion is not too serious. The girls aiming for the lower labor market also fail to support this hypothesis; this failure is serious, and will receive special analysis later.

(2) Those girls fully committed to marriage, without even a curriculum interest to tie current activity with a temporary future in the labor market, should be highly rebellious. And in fact the highest proportion of girls rebellious is in the lower right cell (39 per cent), in correspondence with the hypothesis.

(3) Boys aiming for non-professional sectors of the labor market, and particularly those committed to working class or to no curricula, should be the most rebellious of boys. And they are more rebellious than any group in the table — rebellious students constitute about half of boys oriented toward the lower sectors of the labor market.

(4) In contrast to boys, girls seeking lower labor market positions (mostly secretarial) who are interested in vocational curricula should have good articulation of present activity with future status. Consequently they should be well behaved. Since the comparable subgroup of boys was predicted to be among the most rebellious, the sex-difference in rebellion should be greatest here. The sex-differences in the rate of rebellion are larger in the column of students on vocational curricula than in any other column,[1] in accordance with the hypothesis.

In every respect save one, the distribution of rebellion is as predicted from the theory. But girls oriented to the lower

---

1. Except for the difference involving lower labor market oriented girls without curriculum interest, to be examined immediately.

labor market, without curriculum interest, do not turn out to have behaved very rebelliously (only 23 per cent).

Presumably the situation in which these girls find themselves is relatively transitory, since most of them will probably reorient to marriage. It will be recalled that they *come from* the most conforming group, having been oriented to high positions in the labor market. Perhaps they have not had time to get into trouble, and consequently the indicator used above does not reflect their alienation, for the indicator is a history of rebellion throughout high school, and varies with the amount of time alienated.

We can use reports of amount of homework done, which is a much more short-run behavioral indicator, as a substitute. This avoids the problem of an indicator using a history of rebellion. Since the pattern of boys created no serious problems, and since it remains approximately the same with all the indicators, we will omit boys from the present analysis. The proportion of girls who report doing less than an hour of homework a night is reported in Table 19.

Table 19: Percentage spending less than an hour a day on homework, by image of the future and curriculum interest, for girls.

	Curriculum Interest		
Image of Future	College Preparatory	Vocational	Ambiguous
Labor Market Oriented			
Upper Middle	13% (100)	20% (10)	17% (12)
Lower than Upper Middle	25% (25)	29% (108)	53% (30)
Marriage Market Oriented			
Partly Committed to Marriage Market	21% (70)	35% (106)	38% (47)
Fully Committed to Marriage Market	14% (28)	35% (65)	49% (67)

Here the pattern is clearly as expected. The two highest figures in the table (i.e., the groups doing least homework) are those with low labor market images and no curriculum interest (53 per cent) and those fully committed to the marriage market without curriculum interest (49 per cent). When we remove the problem of the time-span of alienation, the two subgroups expected to be rebellious turn out to be so. Girls oriented to the professional or bureaucratic sectors of the labor market, having good articulation, do their homework. Also, girls partly oriented to the labor market, partly to the marriage market, do their homework. Only those groups of girls who resemble boys in the low amount of status increment they can expect from the school, also resemble boys in the low amount of homework done.

We can also use the attitudes that make up expressive alienation, since these attitude questions also depend less on the time-span of alienation. Thus, more of the girls without curriculum interest, oriented either to the lower part of the labor market or to the marriage market, report that half or more of their classes are boring. About a third (33 per cent and 34 per cent respectively)[2] of these girls with poorest articulation find half or more of their classes boring. Only about an eighth (12 per cent) of the girls with upper middle class aspirations and expectations, and with curriculum interests articulating with such a future, find half or more of their classes boring.

Similarly, we may use the proportion agreeing with the statement that, "You have to get in good with the teachers if you expect to get a fair grade in this school." This indicates alienation from the formal status system of the classroom. Again the highest proportions alienated among girls are those with the poorest articulation.[3] Two-fifths (40 per cent) of the girls oriented to the lower labor market without curriculum interest are alienated from the classroom status sys-

2. Figures in this paragraph are from tabulations not reproduced here.
3. Tabulations not reproduced here.

Table 20: Percentage agreeing that one thing wrong with the school is the number of squares, by image of the future and curriculum interest, for girls.

	Curriculum Interest		
Image of Future	College Preparatory	Vocational	Ambiguous
Labor Market Oriented			
Upper Middle	11% (100)	30% (10)	25% (12)
Lower than Upper Middle	8% (25)	19% (108)	20% (30)
Marriage Market Oriented			
Partly Committed to Marriage Market	7% (70)	22% (106)	47% (47)
Fully Committed to Marriage Market	21% (28)	18% (65)	30% (67)

tem. Thirty-four per cent of the girls fully committed to marriage do not believe teachers are fair. In contrast, only 22 per cent of the girls with best articulation (professional aspirations and expectations, college curriculum) are alienated, and only 27 per cent of the girls aiming for the bureaucratic sector are alienated.[4]

Both alienation from the formal school status system and boredom in classes, then, are most prevalent in the subgroups of girls with poorest articulation. But when we turn to negativistic attitudes, the picture is not so clear. Table 20 shows the proportion of girls agreeing that there are too many "squares" in the school.

The girls oriented to *both* the marriage *and* labor markets

4. In both these tabulations, the largest sex-differences in alienation are between boys with vocational curriculum interests and girls with those interests, in support of the hypothesis. Sex-differences in articulation are greatest here, so sex-differences in alienation should be greatest here.

without curriculum interests are most negativistic (47 per cent agreeing), contrary to the hypothesis. The girls fully committed to marriage, and having no curriculum interest are next highest (30 per cent). But the same girls who failed to be alienated with the indicator of behavioral rebellion in Table 18 again give trouble. The girls oriented to lower positions in the labor market, without curriculum interests, are not very negativistic (only 20 per cent agreeing).

There are several possible *ad hoc* hypotheses that would partially save the main hypothesis, which predicts that these girls will be alienated. The first possibility is much the same as the *ad hoc* hypothesis that was proposed for Table 18. We suggested that these girls had not been alienated long enough to have acquired a rebellious history. Perhaps generalization of alienation from the school to alienation from all conformity likewise takes time. We recall from Chapter 2 that negativism seemed particularly characteristic of boys who had two or more offenses — i.e., a *history* of rebellious activity. It may be, then, that negativism only develops when alienation is long continued.

Second, perhaps the central activities where "squares" become a salient problem to girls are activities in dating. If this is the case, the fact (to be established in Chapter 5) that girls oriented to the labor market but anticipating lack of success in it are less involved in dating would explain the deviant result here. It would also explain why girls partly oriented to the marriage market are highly negativistic, because they date as much as do girls fully committed to the marriage market.

Third, perhaps the term "square" only derives its connotation in active peer group life. The small participation of low labor market oriented girls in dating may reflect general lack of participation in peer culture. If this is the case, the linguistic features of the slang word "square" would explain the deviant result.

In any case, it is clear that negativism (like behavioral rebellion) shows a variant pattern, and only partially supports the hypotheses. In all cases, the hypothesis is supported for girls fully committed to marriage. The group of girls sharing precisely the position of boys, being trapped by an orientation to a labor market that threatens lack of success, are not negativistic and rebellious — but they are otherwise alienated.

By and large, then, the data support the main contentions outlined above. The most rebellious, among both girls and boys, tend to perceive a poor connection between current academic activity and future status. This is indicated by the fact that those who express no curriculum interest are most rebellious and alienated, with other factors constant. It is also indicated by the higher rebelliousness of students aiming for lower positions in the labor market. Further support comes from the fact that sex-differences in rebelliousness are greatest among students with vocational curriculum choices, where the sex-difference in articulation is greatest.

And, though not unambiguously supported, it appears that the subgroups of girls most similar to the larger subgroup of less intelligent boys in articulation, are most similar to them in the degree of alienation. Girls giving ambiguous answers on the curriculum question who are oriented either to low positions in the labor market or to positions not allocated by the school, seem to be most alienated. The only group in which this is not clearly supported is the small number of girls who have lost faith in the likelihood of getting good jobs through a school curriculum but who have not reoriented to marriage. They ought to be expressively alienated. According to some of the indicators they are (not doing homework, short-run hedonism, alienation from the status system), but some of the other indicators do not support the hypothesis (negativism, behavioral rebellion). We advanced *ad hoc* hypotheses to explain these variant patterns, but we do not have data necessary to substantiate them.

SOCIAL ORIGIN, IMAGE OF THE
FUTURE, AND REBELLION

The second indirect argument for the hypothesis of this chapter is that the relation between rebellion and social class is to be explained by the different images of the future taken by working class adolescents. That is, if it is really the future that determines rebellion, then controls by image of the future should eliminate the relation between social class and rebellion. But we must first establish that there is a relation between social origin and rebellion. The material relevant to this is presented in Table 21.

The relation between social class and rebellion is fairly clear for girls. A quarter of the working class girls, but only a sixth of the middle class girls, were rebellious. Among boys

Table 21: Working class boys are no more rebellious than middle class boys; working class girls are more rebellious. Percentage rebellious.

| | | Social Class* | |
Sex	Middle Class	Working Class	Don't Know or No Answer
Girls	16% (195)	25% (441)	28% (32)
Boys	43% (213)	44% (484)	56% (54)

*Students were classified as middle class if their fathers had middle class occupations, or if their fathers went to work "relatively dressed up," or both. Students were classified as working class if they were not middle class by either of the above criteria, provided they gave a manual father's occupation or said he wore work clothes or a uniform to work. If they gave no answer or did not know on both, they were classified as "Don't Know or No Answer." For a possible explanation of the greater rebellion of those who did not answer, see the Appendix on Method, pp. 186-189.

there is virtually no difference (43 per cent of the middle class boys, and 44 per cent of the working class boys were rebellious). The failure of a social class difference to appear among boys is all the more surprising since there is the normal relation between curriculum interest and social origin, and a strong relation between curriculum interest and rebellion. These two relations are presented in Tables 22 and 23.

Table 22: Middle class students are more likely to choose college preparatory curricula, among both boys and girls. Percentage choosing various curricula.

| | Social Class* and Sex | | | |
| | Girls | | Boys | |
Curriculum Interest	Middle Class	Working Class	Middle Class	Working Class
College Preparatory	50%	27%	50%	27%
Vocational	33%	48%	20%	28%
Ambiguous	17%	25%	30%	45%
Total	100% (195)	100% (441)	100% (213)	100% (484)

*See note to Table 21. Students not classifiable by social class have been omitted.

Table 23: Students on college preparatory curricula have skipped school or been sent out of class less often than students on other curricula. Percentage rebellious.

| | Curriculum Interest | | |
Sex	College Preparatory	Vocational	Ambiguous
Girls	13% (223)	26% (289)	31% (156)
Boys	30% (244)	46% (190)	53% (317)

That is, not only does the relation between social class and rebellion, presumably found in the society at large, fail to appear in Table 21; it fails to appear *even though* the articulation hypothesis supports it. This indicates some process creating rebellion which is not considered in either the social class or the articulation theory. By examining the cross-tabulation of these three variables (social class, curriculum interest as a measure of articulation, and sex) with rebellion we may get a clue to its nature. The tabulation is presented in Table 24.

Table 24: Percentage rebellious, by curriculum interest, social class*, and sex.

Sex and Social Class	Curriculum Interest		
	College Preparatory	Vocational	Ambiguous
Girls			
Middle Class	9% (97)	22% (65)	24% (33)
Working Class	15% (121)	27% (211)	34% (109)
Boys			
Middle Class	27% (107)	43% (42)	70% (64)
Working Class	32% (130)	42% (137)	48% (217)

*See note to Table 21. Students not classifiable by social class have been omitted.

Among the boys (who gave the anomalous results above) we find that the working class boys are more likely to be rebellious than middle class boys only if they are interested in college preparatory curricula. Thirty-two per cent of the working class college preparatory boys, but 27 per cent of the middle class boys, have either skipped or been sent out of class. Among the boys with vocational curriculum interests there is no difference between middle and working class boys (43 per cent and 42 per cent rebellious, respectively). But among the group with ambiguous answers to the curriculum question, the relation is actually reversed. Seventy per cent of those from the middle class, but only 48 per cent of those from the working class, have been rebellious.

This suggests that adolescents oriented toward the working class are more rebellious if they originate in the middle class, and vice versa. Some kind of disproportion between the expectations of parents and the student's image of his future may cause rebellion. Still the question remains, why should these disproportions of expectation destroy the relation between alienation and social class in this school, but not in the society at large?

The majority of students on college preparatory curricula in this school are from the working class, so that the school as a whole has an open opportunity structure. This suggests an explanation of the anomalous results in this school.[5] In the society at large, working class students are not as likely to attend schools where opportunities are as open as they are here. Slum schools for depressed ethnic groups sometimes do not even offer serious college preparatory programs. Since the opportunity structure determines the expectations and standards of success, the particularly mobile small town school with little ethnic discrimination would create a different set of success strains than would, for example, the Negro slum school.

Consequently, the relation between social class and expressive alienation (indicated by juvenile delinquency) found in the society at large may be explained by ecological factors. In certain places the relation would hold (large city schools varying in opportunity structure, ethnic groups with markedly different opportunities), and other places it would not

5.   They are similar to the results of F. Ivan Nye, *op. cit.*, pp. 26-31, who also studied small town schools. He also found no relation between social class and delinquency among boys.

(small towns with a single school and therefore a single opportunity structure).[6]

The relation between social class and rebellion among girls fails to disappear when curriculum interest is controlled. In Chapter 6 we will return to the question of the relation between social class of origin, school success, and rebellion, especially to elaborate the implications of social mobility among boys. For the present we will leave the problem, including that of the persistence of the relation among girls.[7]

The analysis thus far is sufficient, however, to support the second indirect argument. The relation of social class to rebellion is weak and unreliable; it does not hold among boys in the school studied, and is actually reversed among boys with poorest articulation of the present with the future. We can therefore regard the second argument for the theory of articulation as being supported, though in an unexpectedly complicated way. Social class enters into the explanation of rebellion in a way very much dependent on the articulation of present activity with future status increment. It apparently affects *both* the future status which students imagine for themselves *and* the degree to which this status is seen as an increment.

6. Natalie Rogoff has shown that at a given level of family status, the highest rate of college planning is in independent towns of less than 100,000 but more than 2,500 people, and in suburbs of more than 2,500. It is lowest in large cities and in rural (2,500 or less) communities. That is, the most open opportunity structures are found in towns in the size range of the town studied ("College, Careers, and Social Contexts," paper delivered at the meetings of the American Sociological Society, September 1959). Further, the presence of an inexpensive college with low admissions standards in the town would further open up the opportunity structure.
7. We may suggest, however, that this failure of the relation to disappear among girls is related to the result of Table 9 in Chapter 2. That table shows that rebellion among girls is strongly related to perception of the school as a status threat to the family, while it is weakly related among boys. This, and the results above, suggest that social class of origin is more salient among girls. Perhaps this is partly due to the fact that it, like the marriage market on which a girl's future depends, is a semi-legal status system.

Evidence in opposition to a long tradition of research and thinking is often either not perceived or is misperceived. It is therefore strategic to emphasize that *there is no statistical relation in this small town, or in others studied by Nye,*[8] *between the social class of boys and rebellion or delinquency.* Much evidence shows that there *is* a relation between social class and delinquency in the society at large. This means that there is evidently some chain of causes between being born of working class parents and being rebellious sixteen years later, and that this chain of causes works differently in small towns than in cities. It works so differently, in fact, that the statistical relation between class and rebellion disappears in some small towns. Note that this does not mean that social class ceases to have any effect on the variables related to rebellion in both contexts. Social class partly determines curriculum choice; curriculum choice partly determines rebellion, *in both small towns and cities.* The reason that this simple chain of causes fails to lead directly to a relation between class and rebellion is that social class determines one's *reaction to* a curriculum choice, as well as determining the curriculum choice.

The lack of association between social class and adolescent rebellion in this small town is sufficient to refute any theory which sees a direct, unconditional chain of causes from birth in a class to deviant behavior in high school. Any such theory is untrue, unless something is wrong with our original data. Social class will be a central variable in the analysis in Chapter 6, but its role in causing rebellion depends on complex intervening processes.

Furthermore, we cannot simply "add" the factor of aspirations and images of the future to the factor of social class, assuming that each generates some rebellion. For if this were the way the causal processes worked, there would be a relation between social class and rebellion in both small

8.   F. Ivan Nye, *loc. cit.*

towns and in cities, but in some small towns there is not. Likewise if aspirations and social class operated additively to cause rebellion, then those of lower social class would be more rebellious regardless of their images of the future, yet among some curriculum groups, those of *higher* classes are more rebellious. A theory connecting social class and rebellion must be complex enough to explain the reason that in some groups of boys, *higher* social class leads to more rebellion.

Also, in this community, social class does not apparently affect the operation of the disciplinary machinery of the school. At the same level of rebellion, students from the middle class are just as likely as those from the working class, but no more likely, to be caught and punished for their rebellion (see the Appendix on Method, p. 203).

ALIENATION AND REBELLION RECONSIDERED

The third indirect argument for the theory of articulation is that it explains expressive alienation, whether or not that alienation has resulted in rebellion. That is, there are students who hold rebellious attitudes who are not behaviorally rebellious, and vice versa. None of the relations between alienated attitudes and rebellion examined in Chapter 2 were perfect. For instance, in Table 8 nearly an eighth (12 per cent) of the well-behaved boys saw the student community as unfair. But viewing the student community thus is more characteristic of rebels, and was consequently inferred to be part of the complex of expressive alienation.

The problem here is to show that the 12 per cent of well-behaved boys who held alienated attitudes have poorer articulation of present activity with future status increment than do the other 88 per cent, whose attitudes were consistent with their behavior.

At the same time, we will try to deal with the converse of this relation. About three-fifths (62 per cent) of the most rebellious boys in Table 8 of Chapter 2 did *not* see the student community as unfair. Even though they have a rebellious history, they may be held not to be as expressively alienated as boys who have *both* a rebellious history *and* the attitudes characteristic of rebels.

In other words, there are random situational factors which determine whether or not a student with a given degree of alienation will be rebellious. The theory developed here *ought not* explain these random factors, for it is a theory of expressive alienation.

In Table 25 we show the relation between hedonism and rebellion on the one hand, and articulation on the other. For a measure of articulation, we have used curriculum in-

Table 25: Hedonistic students have poor articulation, whether they have been rebellious or not, among both girls and boys.

Hedonism and Rebellion	Percentage with Good Articulation	
	Girls*	Boys**
Non-Hedonistic		
Well-Behaved	85% (448)	68% (228)
Rebellious	79% (106)	30% (202)
Hedonistic		
Well-Behaved	58% (69)	16% (92)
Rebellious	40% (45)	11% (130)

*The figures on articulation are not comparable between boys and girls. Girls were considered to have good articulation if they expressed either college preparatory or vocational curriculum interests.

**Boys were considered to have good articulation if their curriculum interest was college preparatory.

terest. Girls were classified as having good articulation if they had either college preparatory or vocational curriculum interests. Boys were classified as having good articulation only if they had college preparatory curriculum interests, in accordance with the analysis above. As long as we do not attempt to compare boys with girls in the table, these different criteria should not confound the analysis.

We have classified each sex into those who said grades were very or quite important to their personal satisfaction, and those who gave some other answer. Those to whom grades were important were considered non-hedonistic; the others were considered hedonistic. We expect that the students who happen to have rebelled will have better articulation than hedonistic students, whether the hedonistic students have rebelled or not.

We see the prediction borne out for both boys and girls. Though rebellious students who are not hedonistic have poorer articulation than students who were neither hedonistic nor rebellious, they have better articulation than hedonistic students, even when the hedonistic students have remained well behaved.

We may carry out the same procedure with the attitude of negativism. By sorting out the negativistic students who have not been in trouble, and the rebellious students who are not negativistic, we can compare that part of the well-behaved population which is more expressively alienated and the less alienated part of the rebellious population. The percentage with good articulation in each of these groups, again using the different criteria for boys and girls, is presented in Table 26.

Again the indirect test of the hypothesis of this chapter is supported. Among both boys and girls, less negativistic students who have a history of rebellion have better articulation of the present with the future than do students who have not been rebellious, but who have expressively alien-

Table 26: Negativistic students have poor articulation, whether they have been rebellious or not, among both girls and boys.

Negativism[a] and Rebellion	Percentage with Good Articulation	
	Girls[b]	Boys[c]
Non-Negativistic		
Well-Behaved	82% (430)	47% (305)
Rebellious	74% (102)	29% (183)
Negativistic		
Well-Behaved	66% (87)	23% (115)
Rebellious	55% (49)	14% (147)

a. Students were considered negativistic if they checked either "Certainly true" or "Probably true" that there were too many squares in the school.

b. Girls were classified as having "good articulation" if they expressed interest in either college preparatory curricula or vocational curricula.

c. Boys were classified as having "good articulation" if they expressed interest in college preparatory curricula.

ated attitudes. The poorest articulation is found in the group whose members are both negativistic and rebellious.

FUTURE AND PRESENT STATUS SYSTEMS

Alienation from the legalistic status system of the Attendance Office follows the same pattern as do the variables above. The well-behaved alienated students have worse articulation than do the rebels who are not alienated.

Thus far, then, the argument of this section is supported. Articulation explains expressive alienation, but not the ran-

Table 27: Students who consider the Attendance Office unfair have poorer articulation, whether they have been rebellious or not, among both girls and boys.

	Percentage with Good Articulation	
Alienation[a] and Rebellion	Girls [b]	Boys [c]
Non-Alienated		
Well-Behaved	81% (471)	44% (344)
Rebellious	71% (115)	25% (240)
Alienated		
Well-Behaved	65% (46)	22% (76)
Rebellious	56% (36)	15% (91)

a. Students were considered alienated from the Attendance Office
if they agreed ("Certainly true" or "Probably true") that the
Attendance Office was "out to get certain people."

b. Girls were considered to have good articulation if they had
either vocational or college preparatory curriculum choices.

c. Boys were considered to have good articulation if they chose
the college preparatory curriculum on the curriculum interest
question.

dom factors which determine whether students at a given
level of alienation get into trouble. When we turn to alienation from the classroom status system, and to the belief that
"you have to get in good with the teachers," certain anomalies appear. The relation between rebellion, alienation from
the classroom status system, and articulation of present and
future, is presented in Table 28.

The expectation of poorer articulation among alienated
well-behaved girls is not borne out, and among boys the relation is actually reversed. Not only are the non-alienated
rebellious boys less likely than the alienated well-behaved
boys to have good articuation; they are actually less likely

Table 28: Percentage with good articulation, by rebellion and alienation from the classroom status system, by sex.

Alienation* and Rebellion	Girls**	Boys**
Non-Alienated		
Well-Behaved	80% (403)	41% (251)
Rebellious	72% (102)	20% (174)
Alienated		
Well-Behaved	75% (114)	40% (102)
Rebellious	59% (49)	25% (157)

*Alienated students agree with the statement that "You have to get in good with teachers to get a fair grade in this school."

**As above, girls are considered to have good articulation if they choose either vocational or college preparatory curricula, boys only if they choose college preparatory.

to have good articulation than alienated rebellious students. And the alienated well-behaved boys have just as good articulation as well-behaved boys who are not alienated. If the argument is to hold up, we must identify a confounding factor which destroys the expected relation, and which must operate especially strongly among boys.

The nature of the anomaly is suggested when formulated in slightly different terms:[9] that college preparatory boys are more likely to be alienated than we would expect. That is, college preparatory rebels are *more* likely to be alienated from the classroom status system than are vocational and ambiguous rebels. And college preparatory well-behaved boys are just as alienated as well-behaved boys among

9. Actually, we are just turning the table around using curriculum choice as the independent variable, and alienation as the dependent variable.

those with vocational and ambiguous curriculum answers. This is clear in Table 29.

Table 29: Rebellious students are more convinced that teachers are unfair if they are college preparatory students. Percentage thinking teachers unfair, boys only.

| | Curriculum Interest | | |
Rebellion	College Preparatory	Vocational	Ambiguous
Well-Behaved	24% (170)	24% (102)	25% (148)
Rebellious	54% (74)	49% (88)	44% (169)
Difference Between Well-Behaved and Rebellious	30%	25%	19%

This is somewhat analogous to the processes we tentatively identified in Chapter 2, explaining sex-differences in alienation from various status systems. We found that girls were more alienated from the highly diffuse status systems, while boys were more alienated from formal systems. The tentative interpretation was that informal status systems were more salient to girls, while formal ones were more salient to boys.

It is possible that grades and classroom status are more salient to college preparatory boys than to vocational and ambiguous boys. Then their greater alienation from classroom status systems is explained by the same hypothesis that guided the analysis in Chapter 2: that alienation is more common among those to whom the status system is most salient, namely college preparatory boys. But this hypothesis entails a further one, that the relation between alienation and rebellion should be stronger among those to whom the status system is more salient than among those to whom it is not. That is, not only should college preparatory boys be more alienated from the classroom status system, but rebellion should also be more closely related to such alienation among them. The last line of Table 29 above reports the differences in alienation between rebels and non-rebels, for the various curriculum groups. We see that the closest relation between rebellion and alienation is among college preparatory boys (30 per cent difference), in accordance with the derived hypothesis. Among those to whom the status system is most salient, rebellion is more closely related to alienation from that system.

Alienation from the formally administered "activities" status system likewise shows anomalies, but this time the deviant results are among girls. (The tabulation is not reproduced here.) In this status system, we may assume that boys on different curricula have about the same amount of investment of themselves, for athletics is not restricted to one curriculum group. But among girls only those who hope to gain status by being leaders in activities would come into sufficient contact with club, dramatics, or newspaper advisors to make this status system salient to them, and such potential members of the "leading crowd" are much more likely to be college preparatory girls.

On the basis of previous reasoning, girls on college preparatory curricula should therefore have much more of themselves invested in the activities status system than do other girls. Consequently the relation between rebellion and alienation should be much stronger in this group than among other girls. Among boys the system is not so differentially salient. so the relation between rebellion and alienation should be about equal. The differences of percentage alienated between rebels and well-behaved students for the sex and curriculum groups is presented in Table 30.

The percentage differences in alienation between rebels and non-rebels are clearly much greater among college preparatory girls than among others. Among boys, as expected, the relation between rebellion and alienation is equally

Table 30: Rebellion is closely related to perception of supervisors as unfair among college preparatory girls, weakly related among boys and non-college girls.

| Sex | Differences in Per Cent Alienated (Rebels Minus Well-Behaved) | |
	College Preparatory	Other
Girls	36%	2%
Boys	19%	15%

strong in both curriculum groups. Among non-college girls, to whom the athletic-activities system is least salient, there is almost no relation between alienation and rebellion. It seems then that the anomaly in this case is likewise due to correlated differences in the saliency of status systems, obscuring the relation between articulation and alienation.

A further test of this explanation for the anomalies in the relation between alienation from status systems and articulation is provided by the question of whether a small clique runs the student community. This test is somewhat more rigorous because we have a rough indicator of the saliency of the student community, namely participation in clubs. That is, if a student participates in high school clubs, we may infer that the student community is a significant reference point for him. And further, if one category has a higher participation *rate* than another category, we can infer that (on the average) the student community is more salient to students in that category. Even if a college preparatory girl and a vocational boy both do not participate, the girl is exposed to the pressures that lead about three-quarters of her peers to participate, while the boy is only exposed to pressures that lead about a third of his peers to participate.

First, we may relate the percentage difference in alienation from the student community between rebels and non-rebels to the participation rates of these categories. This is done in Table 31.

Table 31: In curriculum groups, the higher the proportion belonging to clubs, the closer the relation between aliena- tion from activities status systems and rebellion.

Category	Differences in Alienation from "Cliques" Between Rebels and Non-Rebels*	Per Cent Who Belong to a Club
Girls		
College Preparatory	23%	76% (223)
Vocational	15%	42% (289)
Ambiguous	19%	31% (156)
Boys		
College Preparatory	27%	55% (244)
Vocational	11%	30% (190)
Ambiguous	6%	17% (317)

*Percentage of rebels agreeing that a small group runs student activities, minus percentage of well-behaved agreeing.

Though this relation is not perfect, it is fairly close. The association of rebellion with alienation tends to be highest in the categories whose members commonly belong to school clubs, and lowest when very few of the subgroup are members.

Further analysis is possible if we reproduce the full tabu- lation of sex, rebellion, and curriculum interest and partici- pation by the percentage answering that the student status system is unfair. This imposes a rough saliency control. If, when control by sex, rebellion, and participation is imposed, the percentage alienated increases from college prepara- tory, to vocational, to ambiguous curriculum interest, then the hypothesis is confirmed. For when this pattern appears, then the worse the articulation, the greater the alienation controlling for the saliency of the status system (by controlling participation) and for accidents of getting into trouble (by controlling rebellion). The complete tabulation is presented in Table 32. The numbers, of course, become uncomfortably small in some of the cells, so I have added relevant marginals and consolidated figures.

Table 32: Percentage agreeing that cliques dominate activities, by curriculum interest, rebellion, club membership, and sex.

Sex and Rebellion	Curriculum Interest			
	College Preparatory	Vocational	Ambiguous	Total
PARTICIPANTS				
Girls				
Rebellious	58% (19)	67% (27)	58% (12)	62% (58)
Well-Behaved	39% (151)	50% (94)	46% (37)	44% (282)
Boys				
Rebellious	50% (36)	55% (22)	28% (18)	46% (76)
Well-Behaved	29% (98)	47% (36)	36% (36)	34% (170)
Total Participants	38% (304)	52% (179)	41% (103)	43% (586)
NON-PARTICIPANTS				
Girls				
Rebellious	89% (9)	66% (47)	73% (37)	71% (93)
Well-Behaved	43% (44)	51% (121)	53% (70)	50% (235)
Boys				
Rebellious	71% (38)	62% (66)	50% (151)	56% (255)
Well-Behaved	42% (72)	50% (66)	35% (112)	44% (250)
Total Non-Participants	52% (163)	56% (300)	51% (370)	53% (833)

We may summarize the main characteristics of this complex table by stating that in every case save one, participants are less alienated from the informal status system than are non-participants who are comparable on the other three variables. (In other words, only one figure in the top half of the table is larger than the figure in the same place in the bottom half.) In every case save one, rebels are more alienated than non-rebels who are otherwise comparable. In every case save one, girls are more alienated than boys.

Among participants, who can be assumed to be roughly equal in the saliency of the activities status system, the desired relation appears, that is, those with better articulation are less alienated, controlling for rebellion.[10]

But if we look at the pattern of differences between rebels and well-behaved in the table, we find that the introduction of a rough saliency control has not completely eliminated the differences in saliency we postulated among groups. The imposition of the saliency control (participation) has reduced the size of these differences sufficiently for the hypothesized pattern to emerge in the top half of the table, but the array of differences between rebels and non-rebels in the degree of alienation, by the other variables presented in Table 33, shows that the saliency effect remains.

In each case, the association between rebellion and alienation is stronger in the college preparatory group. Further, it is particularly strong in the categories of non-participants *whose fellow category members most often join clubs.* We may infer that the non-participants giving vocational and ambiguous curriculum responses are non-participants primarily because they are not interested in school clubs. Consequently alienation from the school at large (indicated by behavioral rebellion) is not as likely to include alienation from student activities. The non-participants among college preparatory students, on the other hand, include a larger proportion of those who feel punished by the informal status system. These students are more likely to be alienated from that status system, and more likely to become rebellious.

The other relation established above, that girls are more alienated than boys, is consistent with this explanation. Even

10.   Rebellious boys who participate and who give ambiguous answers depart from the pattern.

Table 33: Differences in percentage alienated from activities status system between rebels and non-rebels are higher for college preparatory students, among both club participants and non-participants.

	Curriculum Interest		
Sex and Participation	College Preparatory	Vocational	Ambiguous
	Differences in Per Cent Alienated		
Participants			
Girls	19%	12%	12%
Boys	21%	8%	− 8%
Non-Participants			
Girls	46%	15%	20%
Boys	29%	12%	15%

when all other factors are controlled, girls base self-conception more on the informal status system. They are, consequently, more alienated.

The failure of the greater alienation of girls from the student community to appear in the gross relations in Chapter 2 may now be better understood.[1] Participation in the informal system decreases alienation. Girls participate more than boys, consequently their greater tendency to be alienated is obscured by this confounding factor. When participation is controlled, girls do appear to be more alienated, as in the original hypothesis.

In each case, then, alienation from a status system is only characteristic of rebels for whom the system is emotionally important. Sex and image of the future determine (partly) the high school status systems in which a student will be primarily involved. Boys are more involved in the formal system, particularly if they are ambitious for professional posi-

1. Compare the discussion of Table 8 in Chapter 2.

tions; girls more in the informal system, particularly if they are ambitious.

We can modify the definition of expressive alienation to include the element of alienation from status systems on which a student's self conception is based, but not all status systems. With this modified definition, the argument that poor articulation explains expressive alienation, whether or not this alienation has resulted in rebellion, is supported by the data.

CONCLUSION

The central hypothesis of this chapter and the preceding one is that expressive alienation can be explained by poor articulation of current activity in the school with future status outside the school. First, we argued that statistics on juvenile delinquency could be organized by the notion that the future status of adolescents was the cause of alienation. We then analyzed why the school as an organization is peculiarly dependent on future status to elicit conformity.

Then we tried to demonstrate that in the group well known to be rebellious, less intelligent boys (i.e., boys headed for the working class sector of the labor market) did in fact have poorer articulation of academic activity with future status increment. Girls, on the other hand, are protected from the career bewilderment characteristic of these boys, because girls can become committed to marriage. They need not aim for unrealistic future statuses, and high school can be meaningful in terms of the transitional labor market.

Those girls who remain oriented to the labor market are almost entirely oriented to sectors of high articulation, the bureaucratic and professional sectors. Boys, even when they chose the lower middle class, aimed for the small business sector where status is not allocated on the basis of education. The curriculum interests of such boys are much more widely distributed than are the curriculum interests of girls oriented toward the lower middle class. This is one indicator of poorer articulation. Our interpretation of the sex and curriculum interest indicators of articulation was verified by a question which asked the students directly how much good jobs depended on grades. Students choosing college or clerical positions thought that grades made a difference in their futures. In developing this argument, we located two subgroups of girls with poor articulation, much smaller than the subgroups of boys. Consequently the first argument of this chapter consisted of showing that these subgroups of girls had, like the less intelligent boys, a high degree of alienation. This prediction was unambiguously successful with the girls fully committed to the lot of housewife, without even curriculum interests to link high school activity to a temporary post-high school job.

But only part of the indicators of expressive alienation and rebellion were successfully predicted for girls still oriented to the labor market but anticipating lack of success, and without curriculum interest. They did less homework, were more hedonisic, and were more alienated from high school status systems than other girls. But they were not more negativistic, nor did they have a history of behavioral rebellion. We advanced the *ad hoc* hypothesis that the failure of both these symptoms of expressive alienation was due to the short time these girls had been alienated.

Second, we tried to show that the articulation of present activity with future status gain explained the association between rebellion and social class. But no such association emerged, at least among boys in the school studied. On investigation, it seemed that social class might affect both the future status of the student *and* the degree to which he saw his status as increment or deprivation. This problem will be investigated further in Chapter 6. However, the irregularity of the relation between social class and rebellion when other factors were controlled is sufficient for the purposes of this chapter. It was only necessary here to discredit the direct social class explanation of rebellion. It is not the case that boys learn to be rebellious in working class families, regardless of their status prospects in school. The influence of social class on rebellion is much more subtle in this school and in those studied by Nye, than in *Elmtown*.

The third indirect argument derived from the fact that expressive alienation as an attitudinal set is not perfectly related to rebellion. This means that there are expressively alienated students who have not yet been in trouble, and there are students who have been in trouble who are not (at least not now) expressively alienated. Since the theory of articulation is a theory of the causes of expressive alienation, it should explain the attitudinal set even when random factors have led students into trouble, or kept them out.

We have now described the phenomenon (namely expressive alienation) to be studied and located its structural context (namely structures which provide poor articulation). But this is not a complete argument. We must still locate the cultural and psychological mechanisms that produce the structural regularities observed.

The incompleteness of the argument is further indicated by the number of loose ends. We have not explained the tendency of rebels to claim adult rights, nor the distribution of expressive alienation by age-grades. We have not explained why social class is not related to rebellion in this school. And the above argument leaves an unpleasant taste of psychological inadequacy—it is hard to imagine adolescents computing status chances in a ten-year distant labor market and then deciding to rebel. We have to reduce the larger social processes to processes of adolescents' immediate experience in order to satisfy our aesthetic sense.

The following chapter deals with adolescent claims to adult rights, the cultural and symbolic processes that yield the structural results outlined above.

5 Adolescent Claims to Adult Status

PSYCHOLOGICAL ASPECTS OF AGE-GRADING

We have so far established that rebellion among high school students is associated with a set of psychological attributes we called "expressive alienation." Further, we have just established that rebellion and expressive alienation are found in subgroups where present performance in formal school activity is poorly articulated with future status, or at least so perceived. In particular, future manual workers are alienated (see Chapter 3, Table 18).

But others besides poorly performing high school students face the future with a self-image as manual workers. Manual workers themselves have relatively little chance for permanently moving into the white collar ranks.[1] And, though they are probably more expressively alienated than white

1. Cf. S. M. Lipset and R. Bendix, *Social Mobility . . ., op. cit.,* pp. 165-169.

collar workers, manual workers seem to be less alienated than adolescents faced with the same future.

To account for the associations established, we have to specify the peculiar situation of the adolescent, his place in the social structure. The syndrome of attitudes and behavior we have named "expressive alienation" is very similar to, though less extreme than, descriptions of defective ego-functioning by psychoanalysts.[2] Consequently, the logical place to look for clues to explain the age-graded distribution of expressive alienation is the field of ego-psychology.

The central problem of the adolescent faced with a universalistic labor market might be called a "constrained choice of identity." It is "constrained" because not all students can perform at the levels required for high status. It is a "choice" because commitments to occupational futures are not fully predetermined before entry into secondary school, and the actual extent of predetermination is concealed by an ideology of equality of opportunity. It is "identity"[3] in the sense that it organizes the commitments of persons to their central roles in public life, and constitutes their claim to specific kinds of treatment by others met in public life.[4]

The special function of the school is to provide public identification according to universalistic criteria. From a subjective point of view, this means that the process of constrained choice involves self-evaluation by universalistic standards. Among the things the student has to learn, then, is the fact that *his parents do not know who he is by uni-*

2. See especially Fritz Redl and David Wineman, *Controls from Within* (Glencoe: The Free Press, 1952). We are only interested in egos defective in the school environment. They may be healthy in other contexts.
3. As used by Erik H. Erikson, "The Problem of Ego Identity," *Journal of the American Psychoanalytic Association*, Vol. 4 (January 1956), pp. 56-121.
4. "The sense of ego identity, then, is the accrued confidence that the inner sameness and continuity are matched by the sameness and continuity of one's meaning for others, as evidenced in the tangible promise of a 'career.' " Erik H. Erikson, *Childhood and Society* (London: Imago, n.d.), p. 228.

versalistic standards. The search for symbols by which to evaluate himself must take place in public life, where the claims made by his chosen identity will have to be validated.

This may be illustrated by brief consideration of some data from the exploratory survey.[5] In a section of that survey a number of statements about the counseling service were provided to half of the student body. Among these was the statement, "I don't think I need much counseling, because I get advice from other teachers or at home."

Among freshmen, 46 per cent of the 91 girls and 37 per cent of the 94 boys checked this statement. Among seniors, only 14 per cent of the 89 girls and 14 per cent of the 96 boys checked it. At first this might be considered merely a gradual realization that parents do not know much about the labor market — but I believe that parents' knowledge of the labor market is regularly underestimated, and that of teachers overestimated. Parents are, on the other hand, poor judges of what their children "deserve" in a universalistic system.

The paraphernalia of the counseling office (psychometric tests, files on students, and the like) and the distinctive expertise of counselors (psychometric testing, *not* labor market analysis) suggest that their function is rather to tell students who they are by universalistic standards.[6] Because parents' judgments of their children are irrelevant to labor market status, the school and the peer group become the central providers of symbols of personal worth. Conversely, in secondary schools, colleges, and graduate schools, everything tends to evolve into a symbol of relative personal worth: personal

5.   This survey was administered early in the year and tabulated by hand with substantial error — see the Appendix on Method.
6.   Of course, the establishment of a center for such universalistic judgments in high school counseling services could be expected to increase the degree to which students' choices are made on universalistic grounds. For instance, the correlation between I.Q. and college plans should be higher in such schools.

habits such as smoking, social relations such as dating and discipleship, achievements such as test scores, term papers, and grades, all become subjectively more important for their identity implications than for their intrinsic worth.[7]

The social structure of schools, on the other hand, tends to reduce the intrinsic meanings of the symbols, to transform them into "merely" symbols of identity, for school activities are distinguished from activities in other organizations by having little effect on the real world. This means that the rewards given to students cannot ordinarily come from benefits brought about by a change in the world, as, for instance, money return from production or honor from victory over real enemies.

This, in turn, means that schools are peculiarly dependent on images of the future as motivating devices. The so-called "rewards" offered by the school are almost all purely symbolic increases in personal worth, symbols supposed to "mean" an increase in future status.

THE SYMBOLIC STRUCTURE
OF SUB-COMMUNITIES: THE HYPOTHESIS
OF RITUAL POVERTY

In working out identity choices, the symbols provided by the formal organization of the school are differentially meaningful according to the type of identity chosen. For those students who form an image of their future in the bureaucratic and professional labor market, the tests, grade averages, and respect of teachers are meaningful ele-

7. For instance, professors often comment on the irritating habit of graduate students to consider their work more from the point of view of what it tells them about themselves, whether they are "brilliant" or not, than from the point of view of what it tells them about the world. This is a reflection of the similarity of structural position between adolescents and graduate students, both being subject to a constrained choice of identity in a universalistic status system.

ments of a *curriculum vitae.* But the formal rituals so appropriate to symbolize advance toward professional status function badly for symbolizing progression toward the "good working class life." Students destined for the working class are (inadvertently) defined negatively in the formal ritual idiom, as "those left over when the middle class is sorted out."

The working class and future housewife subcommunities in the high school find other elements of the culture to use as symbols of identity. These symbols constitute much of "teen culture"; dating, smoking, car ownership, masculinity and aggression, athletic achievement, all can be transformed into symbols of the kind of person one is, or is becoming.

The main symbols of development toward adulthood available to those not aiming for the adulthood approved by the school are symbols not controlled by the formal organization. Claims to smoking, driving, and dating rights cannot be denied completely by the school — they are not supposed to be rights distributed by achievement standards. Attitudes toward objects with which a student defines his place in the world focus around two main poles: the symbol systems permeated with achievement standards (grades, college attendance, etc.) and symbol systems organized around universalistic-ascriptive standards ("adulthood" in general, the sex-division, etc.). Rebellion then reflects the poverty of rituals and symbols that justify subordinate "adolescent" status for the subcommunity of future workers.

THE RITUAL STRUCTURE OF OTHER WORKING CLASS TRAINING

Before analyzing the relations among symbols of adulthood and between them and future status, it may be useful to contrast the ritual organization of the working class sub-community in the high school with a functionally similar subcommunity. Apprenticeship in the crafts is also directed at giving training for a universalistic labor market, and as in high school, the training is supposed to be "generalizable" beyond the firm or school in which training takes place. Like the future worker among high school students, the apprentice is interested in securing a *labor market status* as distinct from a status within the organization.

1. Perhaps the most striking difference between the ritual situations of the apprentice and the future worker in high school is that the apprentice is supposed to be working for a status that not everybody can achieve. Rather than being negatively defined as "left-overs," apprentices are positively identified as future journeymen.

2. Among the mechanisms of this positive identification are the progressive allocation to the apprentice of work defined (in trade union jurisdictional provisions) as too skilled for unskilled workers. The greater command over the skills of the trade is made meaningful by progressive approach to the wages of skilled craftsmen, relatively soon exceeding the wages of unskilled labor.

3. A second mechanism of positive identification of the apprentice is the progressive accumulation of personal capital equipment. The carpenter's apprentice builds a tool kit, buys a set of carpenter's overalls, and so on. The future railroader accumulates a set of standardized clothes, a precision watch, and other portable personal capital. The high school student graduates with a diploma, rather than with a kit of tools.

4. The culminating ritual of apprenticeship is an examination or other test of competence, and the award of a journeyman's card. This is a certificate to future employers of the skill of the workman, and a symbol to the journeyman of the labor market rights he has gained by apprenticeship.[8]

8. "You got a card for that kind of work?" is one of the most commonly heard phrases among craftsmen, both in joking and serious conversation.

The meaning of the journeyman's card is guaranteed by collective contracts which provide that work within the union's jurisdiction can only be allocated to people certified as skilled by the union. The positive meaning of the symbol is indicated by the right generally ceded to the employer of craftsmen to lay off or fire on the basis of incompetence. Such guarantees of the value of the diploma are not provided by the high school. The diploma will be honored by college admissions officers and employers of clerical personnel, but no collective contract (even implicit) generally exists between industrial arts departments of high schools and the employers of manual labor.[9]

The high loyalty of craftsmen to their unions and the unions' superior capacity to provide disciplined labor in industries where firms cannot guarantee careers (e.g., construction) indicate that this system for allocating occupational identities mobilizes personal commitments. The high school is not able to mobilize such commitments from the same population, the future workers.

◆

AN INDEX OF AGE-GRADE ORIENTATION

In order to demonstrate the postulated substitution of ascriptive symbols among the unsuccessful, and to find the other elements of the ascriptive teen culture, it will be convenient to have a slightly more powerful measuring instrument than the single item indicators used in Chapter 2. We may take three of the symbolic claims to adult status for the purpose of constructing a rough index of age-grade orientation: cars, cigarettes, and the right to get married. If students *agree* that a car is necessary to have fun, *do not disagree* that smoking is a student's own business, and say a girl is ready to get married *at less than eighteen years,* they

---

9. In some city trade schools this collective contract does exist. It is also officially supposed to exist in the Soviet Union. We would expect this to mean less alienation among future workers.

may be said to be highly oriented to claiming adult status. If they *do not agree* that a car is necessary, *disagree* with claims to smoking rights, and give eighteen or older as the earliest age at which a girl should consider getting married, they may be said to have an adolescent orientation.

These three items come fairly close to forming a Guttman-type scale, but probably do not satisfy the standard requirements. Therefore we will use that part of the cross-classification that would form a Guttman scale for the main analysis, but we will report statistics summarizing the entire frequency distribution. For upper classmen, with whom we will be mainly concerned, the percentages giving various response patterns to the three items, by sex, are presented in Table 34.

For convenience in labeling tables, I have named the "main scale-types" with numbers, and the other patterns with "E" (for "error") plus a number. Though respondents are only partially ordered, in each case where they are ordered, the number of the adolescent-oriented respondents is less than the number of the more adult-oriented.[10]

If this index does refine the single item indicators of age-grade orientation we used in Chapter 2, the relation between rebellion and age-grade orientation should be greater when this index is used than it was in Chapter 2. In Table 35 the index of age-grade orientation is tabulated against the dichotomous measure of behavioral rebellion. Students are considered rebellious if they have either skipped school with a group of others, or been sent out of class by a teacher, or both.

Concentrating on the "scale types," it is easy to see that the increase in precision of the index of age-grade orientation makes up for the precision sacrificed by dichotomizing the measure of rebellion. Eighty-five per cent of the boys who claim nearly full adult rights (labeled "4" in the table) have either skipped school or been sent out of class or both;

10. See the Appendix on Method for the partial ordering diagram and the statistical tests appropriate for this level of measurement.

only 15 per cent have remained well behaved. In contrast only 29 per cent of the most adolescent boys have either skipped or been sent out; 71 per cent have been well behaved. A similar contrast shows up among the girls. Five-sixths (83 per cent) of the adolescent-oriented girls, and 33 per cent of the adult-oriented, have remained well behaved.

Table 34: Percentages of girls and boys with various response patterns on the index of age-grade orientation, for upper classmen.

	OK for Girls to Marry Young	Do Not Disagree on Smoking	Agree Car Is Right Necessary	Per Cent	Number
GIRLS					
1	–	–	–	50%	235
2	–	–	+	14%	66
3	–	+	+	8%	35
4	+	+	+	5%	24
E1.5	–	+	–	8%	36
E2	+	–	–	10%	47
E3	+	–	+	3%	14
E3.5	+	+	–	2%	10
Total Girls				100%	467

	OK for Girls to Marry Young	Do Not Disagree on Smoking	Agree Car Is Right Necessary	Per Cent	Number
BOYS					
1	–	–	–	24%	131
2	–	–	+	26%	143
3	–	+	+	22%	123
4	+	+	+	7%	41
E1.5	–	+	–	9%	52
E2	+	–	–	3%	15
E3	+	–	+	6%	35
E3.5	+	+	–	2%	10
Total Boys				99%	550

Table 35: Students who claim many adult rights are rebellious; those who claim few are well behaved, among both boys and girls. Percentage well-behaved, for upper classmen.

Age-Grade Orientation and Sex	Percentage Well-Behaved	Number
GIRLS		
1 (Most Adolescent) (−−−)	83%	235
2 (−−+)	73%	66
3 (−++)	49%	35
4 (Most Adult) (+++)	33%	24
E1.5 (−+−)	56%	36
E2 (+−−)	71%	47
E3 (+−+)	43%	14
E3.5 (++−)	60%	10
BOYS		
1 (Most Adolescent) (−−−)	71%	131
2 (−−+)	49%	143
3 (−++)	32%	123
4 (Most Adult) (+++)	15%	41
E1.5 (−+−)	58%	52
E2 (+−−)	47%	15
E3 (+−+)	51%	35
E3.5 (++−)	50%	10

Instead of reporting all the "error patterns" we will report only the "scale patterns" throughout the rest of the chapter, substituting a method of dealing with partial orderings recently developed by James S. Coleman.[1] A set of statistics for summarizing this kind of ordering can be substituted for a report of the complete frequency distribution.

A more detailed summary of this method is found in the Appendix on Method. Briefly, a linear model is fitted to the

1. "Multivariate Analysis," Chapter 6 of *Introduction to Mathematical Sociology* (New York: Free Press, 1964), pp. 189-248.

proportions positive on the dependent variable in a cross classification by the independent attributes. Statistics derived from the model give the effect of each of the independent attributes on the dependent attribute, and provide estimates of random effects in the positive and negative direction.

For example, in Table 35 above, the variation in proportion rebellious may be partitioned into:

Interpretation

$a = .199$ — The effect of not claiming that a car is necessary on the proportion well behaved, controlling for smoking, early marriage claims, and sex.

$b = .169$ — The effect on the proportion well behaved of not claiming smoking rights.

$c = .125$ — The effect on rebellion of claiming early marriage rights.

$a + b + c = .493$ — The effect on percentage well behaved of the three items of age-grade orientation.

$d = .119$ — The effect of male sex on rebellion, controlling for age-grade orientation.

$r = .224$ — The best estimate of the proportion of the "most adult" boys who would be well behaved if the linearity and reliability assumptions of the model were met.[2]

$s = .174$ — The best estimate of the proportion of the "most adolescent" girls who would be rebellious under the assumptions.[3]

---

2.   The actual proportion, as read from the table, is .15.
3.   The actual proportion is $1.00 - .83 = .17$.

Approximately 39 per cent of the possible variation pro-portions in the table is not accounted for by sex and age-grade orientation. Since our analytical purpose is to "ex-plain away" the sex-difference, another 12 per cent of the variation (that part due to sex) is not accounted for *theoretically*. Approximately half (49 per cent) of the pos-sible variation in proportions rebellious is "accounted for" by age-grade orientation, as measured by a partial ordering created by the three items. All three of the items make about equal contribution to the accounting.

ORIENTATION TO THE FUTURE
AND AGE-GRADE ORIENTATION

As we would expect from the analysis above, loyal-ty to the symbols of adulthood is more common among those who do not anticipate achieving high status through educa-tion. Table 36 presents the relation between age-grade orien-tation and curriculum choice, for upper classmen. About half of the students whose symbolic loyalty is to adolescence are on college preparatory curricula. Only about a tenth of those most oriented to early adulthood are "most interested" in college preparatory curricula.

The same pattern shows up with other symptoms of orien-tation to the future.[4] Among girls, 69 per cent of the most adolescent say they have "definitely decided to go" or "prob-ably will go" to college. Only 21 per cent of the most adult-oriented give one of these responses. Among boys, 68 per cent of the adolescent-oriented and 22 per cent of the most adult oriented have definitely or tentatively decided in fa-vor of college. Similarly, 21 per cent of the most adolescent oriented girls both aspire and expect to be professionals, while 8 per cent of the most adult oriented have this vi-

4. The figures in this paragraph are from tabulations not reproduced here.

Table 36: Those who claim few adult rights are likely to be college preparatory students, those who claim many are likely to give ambiguous answers on curriculum interest, among both boys and girls. Percentage choosing each curriculum, for upper classmen, scale types. *

| Age-Grade Orientation and Sex | Curriculum Interest | | | |
	College Preparatory	Vocational	Ambiguous	N
Girls				
1 (Most Adolescent)	46%	39%	13%	235
2	26%	44%	29%	66
3	23%	46%	26%	35
4 (Most Adult)	8%	50%	42%	24
Boys				
1 (Most Adolescent)	51%	24%	25%	131
2	34%	27%	37%	143
3	19%	29%	50%	123
4 (Most Adult)	10%	17%	68%	41

*For the total frequency distribution, the mean differences of proportions college preparatory by the independent attributes are:

$a = .12$ (average difference in proportion college preparatory between those to whom a car is not and those to whom it is necessary)

$b = .14$ (effect of no claims to smoking)

$c = .08$ (effect of no claim to early marriage)

$a + b + c = .34$ (proportion of variation of curriculum choice relevant to age-grade orientation)

$d = .09$ (effect of being male on choosing college preparatory)

$r = .06$ (best estimate of the proportion of most adult girls who choose college preparatory)

$s = .52$ (best estimate of the proportion of most adolescent boys who choose either vocational or ambiguous curricula)

sion of their future. Conversely, only 20 per cent of the most adolescent, but 50 per cent of the most adult girls both aspire and expect to be housewives. Among boys, 37 per cent of the most adolescent aspire and expect to be professionals, while only 5 per cent of the most adult do.

Like perception of personal futures, orientation toward adult symbols is closely related to school achievement. The lower the level of school achievement, the more likely is the transfer of loyalty to ascriptive symbols. Table 37 presents the reported grade averages of students variously oriented toward adult rights.

About half (48 per cent) of the most adolescent girls, but only an eighth (12 per cent) of the adult girls, have a high level of achievement in school. About a third (31 per cent) of the most adolescent boys, but only about a fourteenth (7 per cent) of the most adult, have grade averages of "mostly B's" or better.

It is fairly clear, then, that symbols of early adulthood elicit more loyalty from those students for whom the extension of adolescence is not meaningful, that is, does not lead to the adult status which justifies its extension. When the achievement symbols of identity offered by the formal organization of the school (grades, diplomas, test scores) fail to elicit commitment, loyalty is given instead to the symbols associated with the ascriptive age-grading system (cigarettes, cars, and diamond rings).

THE TRANSFORMATION OF SOCIAL
RELATIONS INTO SYMBOLS

We noted above that in age-graded institutions preparing people for achieved statuses, all aspects of the social environment tend to be transformed into symbols of identity. Social relations, in particular, have strong symbolic overtones.

Table 37: Those claiming few adult rights have higher grades, among both boys and girls. Percentage with various grade averages, for upper classmen, scale types.*

Age-Grade Orientation and Sex	Grade Average		
	"Mostly B's" or Better	Intermediate	"Mostly C's & D's" or Worse
Girls			
1 (Most Adolescent)	48%	47%	4%
2	27%	64%	9%
3	23%	48%	29%
4 (Most Adult)	12%	75%	12%
Boys			
1 (Most Adolescent)	31%	59%	7%
2	17%	66%	16%
3	9%	54%	36%
4 (Most Adult)	7%	41%	51%

*The statistics for the total distribution are, estimating the effect of each of the independent attributes on proportion getting less than a C average:

$a = .03$ (effect of thinking a car is necessary)

$b = .17$ (effect of claiming smoking rights)

$c = .05$ (effect of claiming early marriage)

$a + b + c = .25$ (total effect of age-grade orientation)

$d = .14$ (effect of sex being male)

$r = .00$ (best estimate of proportion of most adolescent girls getting less than a C average)

$s = .61$ (best estimate of proportion of most adult boys getting a C average or better)

The base numbers of this table may be obtained from Table 35.

In high schools, one of the central symbolic social relations is the "dating" relation. The symbolic meaning of dating is closely connected with the age-graded distribution of rights to sexual relations, which are ascriptively allocated to "adults." The Kinsey studies show that the formation of sexual social relations in adolescence is inversely related to the educational and occupational status later achieved.[5]

Conversely, participation in the specifically asexual "activities" of the high school may be said to symbolize the denial of the sexual aspect of social relations among adolescents. The last chapter revealed that this participation was related positively to the status aimed for in the labor market. This finding tentatively supports the interpretation, for we now know that high aspiration is related to both adolescent orientation and to participation in extra-curricular activities. The latter are therefore likely to be related to each other. In Table 38 the frequency of dating is tabulated against age-grade orientation and sex.

About two-sevenths (28 per cent) of the most adolescent girls do not date, while only a twelfth of the most adult girls do not. On the other hand, a little over a fourth (27 per cent) of the most adolescent girls, but three-fourths of the most adult girls, date more than once a week. Among boys, about a seventh of the most adolescent, and about a fourth of the most adult date with high frequency. Conversely, two-fifths of the most adolescent boys, but only about a tenth of the most adult, do not date at all.

Though the propensity to enter into proto-sexual relations is directly related to claims to adult status, the propensity to enter into asexual social relations with peers is inversely related to these claims. Table 39 reports membership in school clubs related to age-grade orientation. Though the re-

5. See Alfred C. Kinsey, et al., "Social Level and Sexual Outlet," in Reinhard Bendix and S. M. Lipset, *Class, Status, and Power* (Glencoe: The Free Press, 1953), pp. 300-308. Both the formation of homosexual and heterosexual relations are delayed for boys oriented toward the middle class.

Table 38: Those who claim fewest adult rights date less frequently, among both girls and boys. Data for upper classmen, scale types.*

	Dating Frequency				
Age-Grade Orientation and Sex	None	Once or Less a Week	More than Once a Week	No Answer	N
Girls					
1 (Most Adolescent)	28%	44%	27%	–	235
2	17%	47%	30%	6%	66
3	20%	45%	34%	–	35
4 (Most Adult)	8%	12%	75%	4%	24
Boys					
1 (Most Adolescent)	41%	45%	14%	–	131
2	24%	53%	20%	3%	143
3	20%	57%	21%	2%	123
4 (Most Adult)	10%	58%	24%	8%	41

*The estimates of the effects in the direction of dating more than once per week are:

$a = .08$ (effect of thinking car necessary)

$b = .10$ (effect of claiming smoking rights)

$c = .17$ (effect of claiming early marriage)

$a + b + c = .35$ (total effect of age-grade orientation)

$d = .28$ (effect of being a girl)

$r = .01$ (best estimate of proportion of most adolescent boys who date more than once per week)

$s = .36$ (best estimate of proportion of most adult girls who date once per week or less)

The application of the sign test for partial orderings shows that, for the left column, there are 7 inversions in 38 comparisons; for the right column there are 3 inversions out of 38. The counting of comparisons is discussed in the Appendix on Method.

lation evidently is not as strong as its converse (dating), it is nevertheless clear that participation in clubs is inversely related to adult claims.[6] Three-fifths (61 per cent) of the most adolescent girls participate, while less than half (46 per cent) of the most adult girls do. Among boys, 52 per cent of the most adolescent and 17 per cent of the most adult participate in school clubs.

Just as relations with peers tend to be transformed into symbols of identity, relations with parents and teachers become symbolic of adolescent or adult status. The subordination required of "children" and "students" is not required of "adults." This ascriptive difference among age-grades can be turned into a symbolic claim to adult status. One index of this transformation of authority relations into symbols of adolescent status is provided by a ranking of several items, among which were "Pleasing my parents" and "Being accepted and liked by other students." Table 40 presents the proportion of students of various age-grade orientations who ranked pleasing parents above being accepted and liked, eliminating the "No Answer" responses and those of the partial answers which do not permit the relative ranks of these two items to be determined.

Again the pattern is not quite as clear as in the case of dating. There is a tendency for the students most loyal to adult symbols to be least oriented to pleasing parents, and most oriented to peer groups. And this is in spite of the greater tendency of the adolescent-oriented to participate in official teen culture and to base their self-respect on their position in that culture. Nearly half (45 per cent) of the the adult-oriented girls, but only a fifth (19 per cent) of the adult-oriented, rank pleasing parents above pleasing friends. Among boys, 60 per cent of the adolescent-oriented, but only 39 per cent of the adult-oriented, rank pleasing parents above pleasing friends.

6. Actually, claims to early marriage rights are slightly positively related to participation in school clubs, while the other two claims are negatively related.

Table 39:   Those who claim fewest adult rights are more likely to be members of clubs, among both girls and boys. Data for upper classmen, scale types. *

Age-Grade Orientation and Sex	Per Cent Members	N
Girls		
1 (Most Adolescent)	61%	235
2	46%	66
3	29%	35
4 (Most Adult)	46%	24
Boys		
1 (Most Adolescent)	52%	131
2	37%	143
3	20%	123
4 (Most Adult)	17%	41

*Estimates of the effects of each of the variables in prediction of the proportion who are members of clubs is:

$a = .18$ (effect of saying a car is not necessary)

$b = .08$ (effect of not claiming smoking)

$c = -.04$ (effect of not claiming early marriage)

$a + b + c = .21$ (total effect of age-grade orientation)

$d = .12$ (effect of being a girl)

$r = .25$ (best estimate of proportion of most adult boys who are members)

$s = .42$ (best estimate of proportion of most adolescent girls who are not members)

Table 40: The most adult-oriented students are more likely to say that "Being Accepted and Liked" is more important than "Pleasing Parents." Data for upper classmen, scale types.*

Age-Grade Orientation and Sex	Percentage Ranking Parents Above Friends	N
Girls		
1 (Most Adolescent)	45%	221
2	54%	61
3	43%	30
4 (Most Adult)	19%	21
Boys		
1 (Most Adolescent)	60%	115
2	46%	127
3	46%	109
4 (Most Adult)	39%	38

*For the total frequency distribution, the effect of each of the independent attributes is:

$a = .10$ (mean difference in proportion ranking parents above friends, between those who do not think car is necessary and those who do)

$b = .03$ (effect of not claiming smoking right)

$c = .08$ (effect of not claiming early marriage)

$a + b + c = .22$ (total effect of age-grade orientation)

$d = .09$ (effect of being a boy in raising the rank of parents relative to friends)

$r = .35$ (random effects toward ranking parents higher)

$s = .34$ (random effects toward ranking peers higher)

Objection to teacher's assumption of authority is more difficult to handle. It is very difficult to separate the objection to teacher authority from the objection to the universalistic standards he is supposed to enforce. Probably behavioral rebellion, shown above to be closely related to age-grade orientation, functions best for this purpose.

In summary, assumption of proto-sexual relations with peers is associated with other symbolic claims to adult status, while the assumption of asexual, "activities" peer relations is associated with an adolescent orientation. Rejection of parental and teacher authority is also associated with loyalty to the symbols of the cigarette, the car, and the diamond. Both relations with peers and relations with adults tend to become symbols of identification.

THE CHOICE OF EGO-IDEALS

Elites in the larger society also have a symbolic function, related to identity choices. It is not possible to develop any complete treatment of the symbolic functions of elites in the general society. For suggestive purposes, however, we may consider certain peculiarities of the military hero as a symbol.

First, the military generally, in modern society, recruits on an ascriptive age and sex basis, especially during wartime. Universal conscription is carried out on the basis of "unachieved" criteria such as age, sex, and physical fitness. Even in the voluntary "hiring" of the armed services through enlistment, criteria of eligibility are not ordinarily the achieved standards which other employers in the youth labor market routinely apply. Second, there is an ambiguous image of the course of military careers in the civilian mind — compounded from the image of the career line of the combat hero, the seniority system, and (more lately) the expert's career line. The distinctive features of the "hero" career line are that the elite positions can be achieved very young, that it is supposedly open to everybody in the armed services, and that it does not require extensive preparation in training centers permeated by achievement standards.

These characteristics of the military, taken together, make the symbolic function of military elites (particularly of the hero variety) especially compatible with alienation from achievement symbols. The nearest approach we have to an indicator of this symbolic area is a structured choice of ego-ideals among boys. Boys were asked, "If you could be any of these things you wanted, which would you most want to be?" They were given a choice between "Jet Pilot," "Nationally Famous Athlete," "Missionary," and "Atomic Scientist." The proportions of boys with various age-grade orientations who chose each of these ego-ideals is presented in Table 41. Boys claiming adult—car, smoking, and marriage—rights are more likely to have an ego-ideal in the most nearly universalistic-ascriptive elite presented to them.[7]

◆

THE SEX DIVISION AND AGE-GRADING

The sex division in orientation to the labor market formed a large part of the explanation of variations in rebelliousness in the last chapter. But just as girls normally win their jobs in a different fashion from boys, they also gain adulthood in a different fashion. The ascriptive symbols of adulthood for boys tend to be rights actively "claimed" by them — cigarettes, cars, rights of sexual access. The ascriptive symbols marking the girls as adults, wedding rings and the like, are "received" by them. The difference in

7. Of course, the position of jet pilot is actually achieved in much the manner of an elite civilian occupation, once the ascriptive recruitment is made. But the details of the status system of the military may not be as familiar to high school students as the achievement standards of athletics and college. And we have forced them to ignore the difficulties by the phrasing of the question.

Table 41: More adult-oriented boys choose "Jet Pilot" as an ego-ideal more often. Data for upper classmen, scale types. *

Age-Grade Orientation	Jet Pilot	Famous Athlete	Mission-ary	Atomic Scientist	No Answer	N
1 (Most Adolescent)	27%	27%	8%	25%	13%	131
2	34%	32%	4%	25%	5%	143
3	45%	25%	3%	20%	7%	123
4 (Most Adult)	49%	27%	—	17%	7%	41

*The effects of the three age-grade orientation variables (sex not being an independent attribute) are:

$a = .08$ (effect of claiming car ownership in raising percentage answering jet pilot)

$b = .02$ (effect of claiming smoking rights)

$c = .07$ (effect of claiming marriage)

$a + b + c = .17$ (effect of age-grade orientation)

$r = .34$ (random effects toward choosing jet pilot)

$s = .49$ (random effects toward choosing other ego-ideals)

ways of gaining adulthood is most clear in the area of sexual (or proto-sexual dating) relations.[8]

This difference in meaning of heterosexual relations is most clear when we consider the implications of dating frequency. We have the paradox that girls date more frequently than boys, yet are less rebellious. This is paradoxical because *within* each sex, those who date more frequently are more rebellious.[9] See Table 42.

8.   The active-passive metaphor is somewhat contaminated by its specialized psychoanalytic use, referring primarily to the physiology of intercourse. I could not think of another adequate metaphor.
9.   It would also be paradoxical if one assumed that high school students only date each other. Boys only date other high school girls, by and large, but girls also date older boys.

Table 42: Girls date more frequently than boys, and rebellious students of either sex more frequently than the well-behaved of the same sex.

Dating Frequency	Girls		Boys	
	Well-Behaved	Rebels	Well-Behaved	Rebels
None	34%	11%	48%	19%
Once a Week or Less	44%	34%	43%	67%
More Than Once a Week	22%	55%	9%	24%
Total	100%	100%	100%	100%
Number	518	145	413	322

The sex-difference in dating frequency is largely to be explained by the orientation of girls to a future as housewives. In Table 43 the percentage of girls dating more than once a week is roughly similar to the percentage of boys, if we consider only girls oriented to the labor market. But orientation to marriage either causes or is caused by more frequent dating.

Since there was evidence that orientation to marriage was associated with relative failure in school achievement, it seems likely that girls oriented to marriage are motivated to enter dating relations, though of course we cannot demonstrate that orientation to marriage came first. That is, if dating frequently of itself fostered reorientation to marriage by causing marriage to appear more desirable or more likely, there seems little reason for orientation to the labor market to be positively related to achievement. On the other hand, the failure of girls oriented to low labor market status to substitute a future as housewife, as a ground for self-evaluation, apparently reflects their relative lack of success in dating. See Table 43.

Dating frequently is not the only claim to adult rights of

Table 43: Girls oriented to marriage, rather than a job, largely account for the greater dating frequency of girls. Data for full sample.

Orientation to Future	Girls	Boys
	Per Cent Dating More Than Once a Week	

Labor Market

	Girls	Boys
Upper Middle on Both Aspiration and Expectation	18% (110)	9% (166)
Lower Middle on Both Aspiration and Expectation	22% (94)	21% (68)
Skilled and Farm, Unskilled, and Tension Between Aspiration and Expectation*	24% (29)	17% (347)
"Don't Know" on Either Aspiration or Expectation	14% (51)	16% (167)

Marriage

Combinations of Occupation and Housewife	32% (231)	
Housewife on Both	44% (153)	

*"Tension" means the occupation aspired to was either higher or lower than the occupation they expected to get.

marriage oriented girls. Orientation to marriage, as expected, increases claims to early adulthood. Thirteen per cent of the 189 upper classmen among girls oriented to the labor market say it would be all right for girls to marry before eighteen years. Twenty per cent of those oriented to both the labor market and marriage give a minimum marriage age of less than eighteen, as do 32 per cent of those fully committed to marriage.[10]

10. From tabulations not reproduced here.

But the other symbols of adulthood, such as cigarettes and cars, are not associated with a claim to early marriage rights as much among girls as among boys. Table 44 reports the percentages of boys and girls of different orientations to the future, who answer that students need cars among those who do and do not claim early marriage.

Table 44: Claims to early marriage do not imply other claims to adulthood among girls. Percentage saying a student needs a car, for upper classmen.

Sex and Orientation to Future	Claiming Early Marriage	Not Claiming Early Marriage
Girls, Labor Market	33% (24)	29% (165)
Girls, Marriage and Mixed	42% (71)	27% (207)
Boys, (All Labor Market)	71% (101)	60% (449)

The ascriptive symbols of adulthood for girls tend not to require active claim. Adolescence for girls, therefore, is not so much failure to achieve adulthood by vigorous action, as it is a period of waiting until someone asks them to get married. Consequently, even the girls oriented to the marriage market find adolescent orientations relatively acceptable.

Let us consider the percentages of girls and boys with the "most adolescent" orientation, classified by their images of the future. We find that the lowest proportion with adolescent orientations among girls is among those fully committed to the marriage market. Thirty-eight per cent of these girls claim no adult rights. (The next most adult is the subgroup giving ambiguous answers, as expected from the analysis of Chapter 4.) The *highest* proportion highly adolescent among boys is in the group oriented to the upper middle class both in aspiration and expectation. But only 42 per cent of them claim no adult rights, practically the same percentage as the most adult group of girls. Boys range down to 25 per cent of the future lower middle class giving a "most adolescent" response pattern, and to 17 per cent of those with visions of a manual future. These figures are lower (i.e., adult claims are more prevalent) than in any subgroup of girls.

In summary, then, we may suggest that the substitution of the marriage market for the labor market reduces rebellion among girls by providing symbols of coming adulthood which are not incompatible with current adolescent status. When boys substitute the ascriptive symbols proper to the adult male role, they claim rights the school is relatively unwilling to grant. Girls substitute claims of the right to make a marriage decision, of which the high school takes little official notice because this claim is generally not cashed in until after graduation.

THE COMBINED EFFECTS OF AGE-GRADE ORIENTATION AND IMAGE OF THE FUTURE

The next question is whether or not either the relation between age-grade orientation and rebellion, or the relation between images of the future and rebellion, are purely functions of each other. The cross tabulation relevant to this question is presented in Table 45.

Only about an eighth (13 per cent) of the most adolescent girls interested in college preparatory curricula are behaviorally rebellious, about a fourth (26 per cent) of the adolescent ambiguous girls are rebellious, and half of the most-adult college preparatory girls are rebellious. That is, there is a certain amount of independent effect of symbolic loyalties and of images of the future. Or, the proportion rebellious increases regularly both as we move to the right, and downward.

A similar pattern occurs among the boys. Boys with vocational or ambiguous answers to the curriculum interest question are more rebellious, controlling for symbolic loyalties. Conversely, those symbolically loyal to ascriptive sym-

Table 45: The percentage rebellious increases with more adult orientations in all curriculum groups, but curriculum groups with poor articulation are more rebellious, at all levels of claims to adult status. Data for upper classmen.*

Age-Grade Orientation and Sex	Curriculum Interest		
	College Preparatory	Vocational	Ambiguous
	Per Cent Rebellious **		
Girls			
Most Adolescent (Scale-type 1)	13% (110)	18% (91)	26% (34)
Intermediate (Scale-type 2 and all error patterns)	17% (40)	38% (84)	41% (49)
Most Adult (Scale-types 3 and 4)	50% (10)	57% (84)	62% (21)
Boys			
Most Adolescent	25% (65)	28% (32)	38% (34)
Intermediate	44% (79)	56% (72)	48% (104)
Most Adult	52% (27)	77% (43)	78% (94)

*If we predict the proportion rebellious, partitioning the effect due to age-grade orientation into two effects (between intermediate and most adolescent, and between most adult and intermediate), and using only college preparatory vs. other curriculum interests, the estimates of the effect of the independent attributes is:

$a = .13$ (effect in raising rebellion rates of a non-college curriculum choice)

$b_1 = .15$ (effect of intermediate compared with most adolescent)

$b_2 = .22$ (effect of most adult compared with intermediate)

$a + b_1 + b_2 = .50$ (combined effect of age-grade orientation and curriculum choice)

$c = .14$ (effect of male sex in increasing rebellion, after controls)

**Having skipped or been sent out or both.

bols are more rebellious, even among boys with the same curriculum interests.[1]

CONCLUSION

The problem of this chapter was to suggest an explanation for the (presumed) age-graded distribution of expressive alienation in modern societies. The suggestion was that the adolescent, exposed through the school to a constrained choice of identity, must make a choice according to achievement standards. When this choice implies an undesirable identity, the formal rituals of the school lose meaning. The school as an organization is peculiarly dependent on the solidity of the meanings of its symbols of identity, because it does not offer real rewards. Organizations whose primary purpose is to modify the environment earn rewards from the environment. What gives meaning to school experience is its symbolic overtone.

The universal secondary school has a formal ritual structure which defines future manual workers as "failures." This ritual structure is in sharp contrast, for example, to apprenticeship systems. Apprenticeship defines working class statuses positively and provides systematic symbols of progression toward them.

When the achievement symbols fail to give a satisfactory self-conception, students substitute ascriptive symbols of adulthood. Cigarettes, cars, marriage, dating relations, participation in activities, relations to parents, school authority relations, and even elites in the society at large tend to be transformed into symbols of identity. Claims to adult status *outside* the formal achievement ritual of the school provide

1. We might suggest that the small number of boys with highly adolescent orientations and vocational curriculum interests are somewhat comparable to the "boys" in the apprenticeship system. If the vocational curriculum is meaningful to them, then the teacher's authority is acceptable.

a meaningful self-conception for those to whom the adolescent self-conception is undesirable. Adolescence comes to be undesirable to students whose future is not attractive enough to justify current subordination.

The sex division, by providing different types of symbols of adulthood to boys and girls, allows girls to give loyalty to ascriptive symbols which *are* compatible with current adolescent status. Even girls who have substituted the semi-ascriptive marriage system are less likely than boys to claim other adult rights actively — even when they do claim the right to early marriage. This seems to explain why girls, who date more frequently than boys, are less rebellious, even though within the sexes those with higher dating frequency are more rebellious. Girls dating frequently and claiming early marriage *are* claiming adult rights, but they can claim them passively.

Finally, it seems that loyalty to the ascriptive symbols of adulthood (cigarettes, cars, and diamonds) is associated with rebellion even when orientation to the future is controlled. The perception of the symbolic features of the school environment itself has an effect, independent of the career meaning of the school.

The overall conclusion is that commitment to the culture of ascriptive symbols of identity is a reaction against the ritual inadequacy of the achievement symbols which form the culture of the formal organization. By motivated transfer of loyalties from one cultural system to another, the students reduce the punishment to their self-respect involved in loyalty to achievement symbols. The more active this claim to adult status, the more active is the rebellion against the organization bearing achievement symbols. The cultural aspect of high school rebellion is made up of the symbols of adulthood generally prevalent in the society. But only the strain imposed on students by the achievement system can explain the pattern of differential loyalty to these symbols, seen especially in Table 37.

The final problem is why lack of commitment to the school, apparently explained by lack of career meaning of formal school activity and by the substitution of other symbols, takes the form of active rebellion. It would be possible for such a lack of commitment to result in apathy, rather than rebellion.[2] For this purpose, we will use some aspects of the theory of deviant behavior developed consequent to Robert K. Merton's paper on "Social Structure and Anomie."[3]

2.   For a case, see Erik Erikson's analysis of the apathy of the Sioux Indians in *Childhood and Society, op. cit.*, pp. 98-140.
3.   *Loc. cit.*

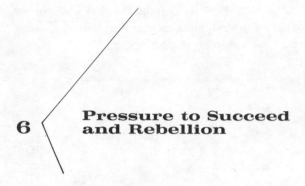

6 | **Pressure to Succeed and Rebellion**

The assertion of the theory of "Social Structure and Anomie" is that the distribution of deviant behavior in modern society can be explained by the following propositions: (1) the universality of the criterion of "success" in the economic system (especially the labor market) subjects to the same standards people who have different opportunities to succeed; (2) those subject to the greatest strain between success goals and legitimate opportunities to succeed are especially likely to lose their commitment to either the goals, or the means, or both; (3) types of deviant behavior vary according to which is rejected: (a) rational, organized crime is an example of lack of commitment to legitimate means, (b) ritualistic observance of the forms of the competitive struggle, whether or not it leads to success, is an example of lack of commitment to success goals, (c) apathy normally involves rejection of both the goals and the means, and (d) rebellion normally involves ambivalence toward both goals and means.[1]

The school system, particularly the secondary school, is one of the main institutions in the society where universal standards of success are applied over the whole range of the class system. Students are placed under great pressure to force a decision on the degree of success they expect, and the (symbolic) means of success, especially grades, are deliberately and systematically allocated differentially. Further, the ritual idiom of the school, by defining only middle class choices positively, allows but a very limited redefinition of the meaning of "occupational success." Apprenticeship systems, on the other hand, have a ritual structure tending to define manual work as occupational success.

As suggested in the last chapter, punishing self-evaluations in the achievement system of the school tend to result in the substitution of alternative systems of self-evaluation, especially ascriptive ones. But these tend to be differentially available and differentially convincing substitutions. Marriage seems to be a more effective alternative than the adult consumption pattern available to boys. Marriage can be a real future, giving meaning to current activity, while the consumption pattern of male adults really promises little but lung cancer.

Aside from the differential opportunities to substitute other standards, standards of occupational success are differentially incorporated into the personalities of students. Normally we would expect that the school's ritual idiom, defining occupational success in middle class terms, would have greatest resonance among middle class children. Of course, middle class children are also more likely to have access to the means of success, by being more intelligent and better

1. From a psychological point of view, then, rebellion would be considered a "reaction formation," where the violence of rejection of success goals and of the norms of competitive struggle depends on their previous introjection.

trained for the competitive struggle. But there is an essential distinction between *personal* means of success (intelligence, physical beauty, and the like) and *social* means (parental culture, money, grooming, social contacts). Social means of success tend to be highly correlated with social class, and hence with pressure to succeed, but the correlations between parental social status and personal means of success, though positive, are not as high.

There are thus many intellectually ill-equipped boys under great pressure to succeed, and bright boys who lack the social means of success. Very likely both types of disproportion tend to produce rebellion. In this high school, as the following analysis will show, the pressure to succeed on all boys, even from the working class, is quite great regardless of ability. The prospects of the bright boys from the working class are apparently sufficiently promising to make them more conformist than their non-mobile working class peers. But they are less conforming than non-mobile middle class boys, due to their lack of *social* means of success.

The main burden of the analysis, however, falls on those boys who are under great pressure to succeed from their parental and neighborhood environment, but who are intellectually ill-equipped for academic competition. Middle class students who are unsuccessful in school would be under exceptionally great strain. We saw in Chapter 4 that such students seem to be somewhat more rebellious. Our purpose is to refine this analysis.

◆

THE DECISION NOT TO SUCCEED

One reflection of the internalization of success goals is the decision to get further education. A good many studies have shown that at a given intelligence and achievement level, high school students from the higher social classes are more likely to decide to go on to college. Yet the converse of this process, *the incapacity to decide not to go to college*, has been little analyzed. If success goals are internalized, if a student judges himself by middle class standards, he should have a very difficult time resigning himself fully to lack of success.

To secure a measure of the degree of pressure to succeed, we assign the students by class level into upper middle class, lower middle class, and working class. Since the logging and sawmill industry is characterized by a good many very small firms in which the owner does manual work, I decided to use a combined criterion of occupational classification and the type of clothes worn to work. Professionals, businessmen, and government officials who go to work "relatively dressed up" are classified as upper middle class. All clerks and salesmen, and professionals or businessmen who wear work clothes or uniforms, and those few whose occupation is manual or farm but who wear dress clothes, are classified as lower middle class. Those whose occupation is manual or farm, and who wear work clothes or uniforms to work, are classified as working class.[2]

I believe that this combination of occupational and symbolic criteria fits the particular class structure of the town about as well as more complex criteria.[3] Reputational rankings would be considerably confused by the urban-like anonymity of the community. Purely occupational rankings would not distinguish the large working businessman element from the middle class proper.

In Table 46 we present the college decisions of students grouped by grade average, social class, and sex. It is clear

2. If a professional's or businessman's clothes are not described, he is placed in the lower middle class. If a worker's clothes are not described, he is placed in the working class. If an occupation is not given, those who dressed up were put in the lower middle class, and those who wore work clothes were put in the working class.
3. See William H. Form and Gregory P. Stone, *The Social Significance of Clothing in Occupational Life*, Technical Bulletin 247 (East Lansing: Michigan State University, 1955).

Table 46: Percentage definitely decided to go to college, undecided, and definitely decided *not* to go, by social class, grade average, and sex.

Sex, Grade Average, Social Class	Definite, Yes	Unde- cided*	Definite, No	N
GIRLS				
"Mostly B's" or Better				
Upper Middle	75%	18%	7%	40
Lower Middle	67%	30%	3%	61
Working	54%	35%	12%	138
Total with High Grades	61%	31%	9%	239
"Mixed C's and B's" or "Mostly C's"				
Upper Middle	59%	36%	5%	22
Lower Middle	38%	39%	23%	61
Working	22%	47%	31%	268
Total with Intermediate Grades	27%	45%	28%	351
"Mixed C's and D's" or Worse				
Upper Middle	**	**	**	--
Lower Middle	**	**	**	4
Working	10%	34%	56%	62
Total with Low Grades	11%	33%	56%	66
BOYS				
"Mostly B's" or Better				
Upper Middle	93%	7%	--	29
Lower Middle	75%	25%	--	32
Working	68%	28%	4%	81
Total with High Grades	75%	23%	2%	142
"Middle C's and B's" or "Mostly C's"				
Upper Middle	55%	45%	--	22
Lower Middle	53%	34%	13%	79
Working	28%	54%	18%	302
Total with Intermediate Grades	34%	50%	16%	403
"Mixed C's and D's" or Worse				
Upper Middle	**	**	**	3
Lower Middle	17%	61%	22%	36
Working	12%	47%	41%	150
Total with Low Grades	13%	50%	37%	189

*"Undecided" includes "Probably will go," "Probably will *not* go," "Don't Know," and No Answer.
**Too few cases for meaningful percentages.

that all three variables are independently related to the college decision. Boys, higher grade-average groups, and higher social classes are more likely to decide to go to college.

But we are particularly interested in the figures in the right hand column (the "Definitely Decided Not to Go" responses). The important features of this column may be presented separately for convenience. In Table 47 we present the proportion decided not to go to college among those with less than C averages. The only groups with sufficient numbers of students with less than C averages are working class girls, working class boys, and lower middle class boys. Probably few of these students will go to college and probably none will secure professional positions in the labor market. The proportion resigned to this dismal future is relatively small, but it is more significant for our purposes that boys are less resigned than girls, and middle class boys are less resigned than working class boys.

Table 47: Boys, especially middle class boys, do not decide not to go to college, even among students with less than C averages. *

Sex and Social Class	Percentage of Unsuccessful Decided Not to Go
Working Class Girls	56% (62)
Working Class Boys	41% (150)
Lower Middle Class Boys	22% (36)

*Source: Table 46.

Another way of looking at the same phenomenon is to examine the amount of influence of academic success on the decision not to go to college. Subtracting the percentage decided not to go to college among the successful (grades B or better) from the percentage not going among the failures (less than C average) gives a measure of willingness to be convinced that one is not college material. The greater the difference in decisions, the greater the willingness to accept the implications of academic failure. As seen in Table 48, girls are more swayed by grades than boys; working class boys are more influenced than middle class boys.

Table 48: Grades make less difference in the decision of boys not to go to college, especially middle class boys, than in the decision of girls. *

Sex and Social Class	Difference Between Successful and Unsuccessful in Percentage Decided Not to Go**
Working Class Girls	44%
Working Class Boys	39%
Lower Middle Class Boys	22%

*Source: Table 46.

**High differences indicate greater willingness to be convinced that one is not college material.

What happens, then, to the college plans of students unwilling to fail, but unlikely to succeed? Table 49 shows that

Table 49: Grades make no more difference among girls than among boys in the decision definitely to go to college. *

Sex and Social Class	Difference Between Successful and Unsuccessful in Percentage Decided to Go**
Working Class Girls	44%
Working Class Boys	56%
Lower Middle Class Boys	58%

*Source: Table 46.

**The higher the difference, the greater the effect of grades in convincing students that their college aspirations are not certain.

lack of academic success is sufficient to convince students in all categories that positive college plans cannot be made, reporting the differences in percentages definitely decided *to go* to college, between successful and unsuccessful students.

Low grades are sufficient in all groups to convince students that their success is not certain. The unsuccessful boys, especially the lower middle class boys, caught between the conviction that they are not certain to succeed, and an unwillingness to fail, are pushed into the "undecided" category. The percentage undecided among the academically unsuccessful, by sex and social class, is presented in Table 50.

The indecision of lower middle class boys who are academically unsuccessful, then, seems to reflect a conflict between two pressures. On the one hand, the school is attempting to convince them that they are unlikely to succeed; on the other, their sex and class position makes it very punishing for them to fail. Working class boys find it hard to fail, but not as hard as lower middle class boys; working class girls find it easiest to fail.[4]

It should be noted, however, that it is not really easy for any of the subgroups to abandon the idea of labor market success. Even among girls from the working class with low

4.   Originally I had intended to use indecision itself as an indicator of this conflict between success pressures and restriction of the means. As may be seen from Table 46, the next highest percentage undecided (after lower middle class failures) is among working class boys with intermediate grades (54 per cent undecided). If we assume that workers' sons are generally under less pressure to succeed (as indicated by the data above), then the situation of these undecided is opposite to that of the lower middle class failures. Their indecision can be interpreted as questioning whether the *promises* of success in school are sufficient to leave behind their more comfortable working class level of aspiration. The lower middle class failures have to decide whether the *lack of promises* from the school is sufficient to keep them from living up to their parental culture. The meaning of indecision for attitudes toward the school is opposite for these groups differently situated in the social structure. Consequently indecision itself is a poor indicator of the status threat of the school.

Table 50: Academically unsuccessful lower middle class boys are highly undecided about college plans. Percentage undecided among academically unsuccessful students, by social class and sex.*

Sex and Social Class	Percentage Undecided
Working Class Girls	34% (62)
Working Class Boys	47% (150)
Lower Middle Class Boys	61% (36)

*Source: Table 46.

grades, only a little over half have definitely decided not to go to college. Since we can predict from our knowledge of colleges and of the class system that of these girls actually very few have any chance of going, this is still a major mis-evaluation of their chances. A tenth of them have "Definitely decided to go to college," which is probably more than will actually go.

The basic hypothesis of this chapter is that high commitment to success combined with actual failure produces rebellion. More specifically, students most subject to self-evaluation by standards of occupational success are lower middle class boys; those next most subject to such self-evaluation are working class boys; those least subject to such self-evaluation are girls. Though we assume that lack of success is punishing to all, it is *most* punishing to middle class boys, *next most* punishing to working class boys, and *least* punishing to working class girls. Consequently we expect to find rebellion among the unsuccessful more than among the successful, more among the male unsuccessful than among the female unsuccessful, and more among the middle class unsuccessful males than among the working class unsuccessful males.

◆

STRAIN AND REBELLION

The empirically specified hypothesis is that rebellion will be most characteristic of boys who are unsuccessful in school and who come from middle class homes. The
data relevant to this hypothesis are presented in Table 51.

Table 51: Percentage rebellious, by grade average, social
class, and sex.

	Social Class		
Sex and Grade Average	Upper Middle	Lower Middle	Working
Girls			
High Grades[a]	8% (40)	18% (61)	18% (138)
Intermediate[b]	18% (22)	18% (61)	26% (268)
Low Grades[c]	* (−)	* (4)	39% (62)
Boys			
High Grades	7% (29)	19% (32)	25% (81)
Intermediate	27% (22)	49% (79)	43% (302)
Low Grades	* (3)	83% (36)	60% (150)

a. "High Grades" denotes "Mostly B's" or better.
b. "Mixed B's and C's" or "Mostly C's."
c. "Mixed C's and D's" or worse.
*Too few cases for meaningful percentages.

Among the academically unsuccessful boys, 83 per cent
of those from middle class homes, but only 60 per cent of
those from working class homes, have either skipped school
or been sent out of class, or both. (Similarly, in the intermediate grades group, boys from the lower middle class
are slightly more likely to have been rebellious.)

Further, both these figures are considerably higher than
the percentage rebellious among unsuccessful girls (39 per
cent). That is, it appears that lack of academic success
causes rebellious behavior most often among precisely the

groups who find it most difficult to decide not to succeed. Finally, in accordance with the hypothesis, academic success makes more *difference* in rates of rebellion among boys, especially among middle class boys. See Table 52.

Table 52:   Grades make more difference in the rate of rebellion among boys, especially lower middle class boys.*

Sex and Social Class	Difference Between Successful and Unsuccessful in Percentage Rebellious
Working Class Girls	21%
Working Class Boys	35%
Lower Middle Class Boys	62%

*Source: Table 51.

Of course there is a distressingly small number of cases (thirty-six) in the cell expected to be the most highly rebellious. Furthermore, the reaction of lower middle class boys to failure is crucial to the argument. This is the only place in the table above where the mechanism suggested gives different results than would be predicted by the notions outlined in previous chapters. It is, for that matter, the only place where a simple linear relation between both social class and grades (controlling for sex) fails to account for rebellion.

Because of the small number in the crucial cell, the remainder of the chapter will consist of indirect argument in support of the main contention. First, we will show that the lower middle class academic failures are more alienated by a whole series of criteria. This gives confidence that the result above is not merely an accident of the history-of-rebellion criterion. Second, we will consider two other ways of measuring strain, in an attempt to show that these, too, support the hypothesis, although these indicators tend to give small and erratic results. We will merely list a number of other measures of strain which also give either small or erratic results. We will then attempt to explain why analysis by social class and academic failure is successful, while other indicators do not function very well.

This procedure will, of course, leave the hypothesis in a weak condition. The final sections of the chapter attempt to state some alternative hypotheses that have been suggested to explain the same set of facts. We will try to show that these alternatives are also feeble, being either refuted or shown to be insufficient by the data. We will hold that our weak hypothesis, partly supported, is worth investigation, since the alternatives are also weak and partly refuted. Lines of research that might help decide the question will be suggested.

◆

STRAIN AND ALIENATION

Because it would be tedious to construct and read the full tables in order to analyze the behavior of a single cell, we will report only the "toughest" comparison — that between lower middle and working class boys with low grades. The prediction is that lower middle class unsuccessful boys will be more alienated than comparable working class boys.

The other behavioral indicators of alienation, cheating and amount of homework, give relatively poor results. Thirty-nine per cent of the (36) lower middle class boys, and 35 per cent of the (150) working class boys among those with low achievement, report having cheated within the past month. Twenty-two per cent of the lower middle class boys answer "Don't Know," while only 10 per cent of the working class boys say "Don't Know" (and 4 per cent fail to respond). Presumably, answering "Don't Know" indicates less behavioral commitment to the norms than answering that one did not cheat. If we count both "Don't Know" and "No Answer" as indicating cheating, then 12 per cent more lower middle class boys indicate propensity to cheat than do working class boys. Since these interpretations of the meaning of ambiguous responses cannot be verified, we must conclude that this indicator does not give clear results.

Sixty-nine per cent of the lower middle class unsuccessful boys and 70 per cent of the working class boys report doing less than an hour's homework a day. Though these proportions are about the same, failures to give a definite answer may account again for the smallness of the difference. About a seventh (14 per cent) of the lower middle class boys, but only 2 per cent of the working class boys, failed to answer the question on the amount of homework.

Though these indicators do not show lower middle class boys more rebellious, they at least do not clearly disprove the hypothesis. Turning to the attitudinal indicators, the items indicating a short-run hedonistic attitude toward school show lower middle class failures more alienated than working class failures.[5] Nearly half (47 per cent) of the lower middle class unsuccessful and only two-fifths (39 per cent) of the working class unsuccessful say that half or more of their classes are "pretty boring." A quarter (25 per cent) of the lower middle class unsuccessful, and 23 per cent of the working class unsuccessful say that grades are "very important" to their own satisfaction. Thirty-three per cent of the lower middle class and 32 per cent of the working class boys say it doesn't matter how hard one works in a class.

We find similar results with the indicator of negativism. About three fifths (58 per cent) of the relevant lower middle class boys, and about a half (51 per cent) of the working

5.   We intend to use a sign test to summarize all the attitudinal indicators. Consequently, we will count small differences as either confirming or contradicting the hypothesis.

class boys say that there are too many "squares" in the school.

The percentages for the items indicating alienation from the status systems may be presented in tabular form:

Type of Alienation	Lower Middle Unsuccessful	Working Class Unsuccessful	Difference
Agreeing Attendance Office Is Unfair	28%	37%	− 9%
Agreeing Teachers Unfair	53%	41%	+ 12%
Agreeing Coaches Unfair	69%	57%	+ 12%
Agreeing that Small Group of Students Run Things	50%	49%	+ 1%
Agreeing that Parents Feel Uncomfortable at School and PTA	53%	42%	+ 11%
Number	**36**	**150**	

Only the item on the Attendance Office is inverted. In other cases, failing students from the lower middle class are more alienated than students from the working class.

Of the age-grade orientation items, half show the academically unsuccessful from the lower middle class more oriented to becoming adults, while the other half show those from the working class more adult oriented.

In summary, the two other behavioral indicators (cheating and doing very little homework) do not give clear results. Of the seventeen relevant attitudinal items, twelve show the academically unsuccessful lower middle class boys to be more expressively alienated. Of the minority of five

Item of Age-Grade Orientation	Lower Middle Unsuccessful	Working Class Unsuccessful	Difference
Agree Students Need Care	81%	73%	+ 8%
Agree Smoking Is Student's Own Business	53%	47%	+ 6%
Owns Car	53%	34%	+19%
Dates More than Once Per Week	28%	17%	+11%
Approves Early Marriage for Girls	22%	29%	− 7%
Does **Not** Belong to School Club	81%	81%	− 0%*
Ranks "Being Accepted and Liked by Other Students" as More Important than "Pleasing My Parents"	41% (N = 29)	51% (N = 130)	− 10%**
Chooses "Jet Pilot" as Ego-Ideal	42%	48%	− 6%

*The working class unsuccessful participate less by 0.1%.

**Due to the physical setup of the questionnaire, many students checked their first choice rather than ranking the items. We used only those where the relative ranks of the two items could be determined.

items showing boys from the working class to be more alienated, four concern loyalty to ascriptive symbols of adulthood. Perhaps the age-grade orientation of working class parents is enough different than the orientation of middle class rents to cause these inversions.

At any rate, the weight of the evidence from the other indicators of expressive alienation is on the side of the hypothesis. We can therefore assume that it was not unreliability of the history of rebellion which gave us the results. The group of lower middle class failures is more alienated by a whole series of indicators, with different cutting points.

◆

OTHER INDICES OF STRAIN

Another way to check the reliability of this result would be to change the indicators of strain between success goals and access to the means. That is, if strain between success goals and access to the means does create rebellion, the results should be consistent with any of several indicators of strain. If only one of the indicators (for instance, disparity between class of origin and grade average) gives the expected result, while others do not, then the supporting evidence may be a statistical artifact. Or it may be due to some other process.

One such alternative index was reported in Chapter 4, when we noted the inversion of the relation between social class and rebellion among the different curriculum groups. Students giving ambiguous curriculum answers were more likely to be rebellious if they came from the middle class. The evidence from Chapter 4, then, supports the hypothesis.

Similarly, we may use images of the future as indicators of success, and suppose that among the students who envision themselves in low occupations, those from the higher social classes will be more rebellious. The relevant tabulations are presented in Table 53.

The pattern of this table works out as expected, if we simply contrast the lower middle class with the working class. Among boys, who do not have either the marriage or the clerical alternatives to professional futures, those who choose lower are more rebellious (60 per cent) if they come from the lower middle class. But we expect that the most rebellious of all would be those from *upper* middle class homes who anticipate being downwardly mobile. Actually this group is the least rebellious of any of the subgroups of boys. It is all sufficiently perplexing.[6]

Two *ad hoc* hypotheses might explain this deviant pattern of upper middle class boys. First, the upper middle class may not actually exert as much pressure as the lower middle class. Second, the upper middle class family may be more capable of dealing with or alleviating the strain imposed. We will deal with these alternatives in turn.

The answers to the question, "Do your parents urge you to go to college and to take college preparatory subjects in high school?" should indicate success pressures from the families. Table 54 shows that these success pressures vary directly with social class, even among those who do not envision themselves as professionals.

The girls oriented to the lower sectors of the labor market show a variant pattern, but there are only nine cases in the upper middle class cell. Otherwise the relation is perfectly consistent. The higher the social class, the higher the pres-

6. Data from a study by James S. Coleman gives the same anomalous pattern:

Percentage answering that they smoked and drank beer and drank liquor, at least occasionally, by social class and curriculum interest, for Midwestern boys.

| Curriculum Interest | Social Class * | | |
	Upper Middle	Lower Middle	Working
College Preparatory	6% (448)	9% (443)	10% (709)
All Other Answers	12% (161)	19% (325)	15% (1388)

*"Upper Middle" includes sons of professionals and high status proprietors, managers, and officials. "Lower Middle" includes clerical and sales workers, and low status proprietors, managers, and officials, but not those proprietors who primarily work rather than manage an enterprise. "Working" class boys are sons of men in manual occupations, and sons of those proprietors who mainly work with their hands (e.g., including family farmers).

sure to succeed, even among those not aiming for professional positions.[7]

Other indirect evidence of the parental pressure is the
rate of substitution of the marriage market as a system of
self-evaluation among girls. We would hypothesize that if
the pressure is greater in the upper middle class, then upper middle class girls *without* professional aspirations would
be most likely to substitute the marriage market, while girls
from the working class would find it easier to accept lower
positions in the labor market. Table 55 presents the percentages of those without professional images of their future who
mention housewife on at least one of the questions of aspira-

7. Incidentally, this tabulation supports and extends the results of Joseph A. Kahl, "Educational and Occupational Aspirations of 'Common
Man' Boys," *Harvard Educational Review,* Vol. 23 (1953), pp. 186-
203. Kahl found that among boys in the middle ranges of the social
class system with high I.Q.'s, parental urging was the central determinant of the college decision. We find this same relation both in the
middle of the class ladder and in its upper reaches. The influence
of parental urging on the college decision and occupational aspiration
emerges even more clearly if we consider the percentages reporting
that parents "strongly urge" college planning. In each social class,
the proportion reporting strong urging is much greater among those
who envision professional futures.

Strong college urging by parents greatly encourages professional aspirations and expectations, in all social classes,
both sexes. (Base numbers may be obtained from Table 54.)

Sex and Social Class	Image of Future		
	Upper Middle	Lower than Upper Middle	Marriage
	Per Cent Reporting Strong Parental Urging		
Girls			
Upper Middle	71%	22%	38%
Lower Middle	46%	36%	25%
Working	31%	16%	12%
Boys			
Upper Middle	70%	29%	
Lower Middle	50%	25%	
Working	41%	16%	

Table 53: Percentage rebellious, of students from various
social classes with various images of the future, by sex.

	Image of Future		
Sex and Social Class	Upper Middle[a]	Lower, Labor Market[b]	Marriage[c]
Girls			
Upper Middle	− − (21)	22% (9)	16% (32)
Lower Middle	8% (26)	10% (29)	24% (71)
Working	19% (62)	25% (132)	27% (274)
Boys			
Upper Middle	17% (23)	16% (31)	
Lower Middle	30% (44)	60% (103)	
Working	34% (98)	47% (435)	

a. Choosing upper middle class occupations (Professional, Entertainer, and Airline Stewardess — very few of the last two) as
both aspiration and expectation.

b. Choosing occupation lower than upper middle class on either
aspiration or expectation or both, with neither aspiration nor
expectation "Housewife."

c. Either aspiration or expectation or both "Housewife."

tions and expectations. This indirect test also supports the
hypothesis that upper middle class families put more pressure on adolescents than do lower middle and working class
families.

Finally, we may refer again to Table 46, on the capacity
for students of different social classes to decide not to go to
college. In each case those from the upper middle class
found this decision more difficult.

The alternative *ad hoc* hypothesis that upper middle class
failures were not rebelling because they are not subject to
success pressure is contradicted by the data. We may consider the second *ad hoc* hypothesis. It may be that upper
middle class families are able to delay the identity crisis until after high school, while lower middle class boys are forced
to decide on their level of success during high school. The

upper middle class family has to deal only with a moderate level of failure — the chance of the adolescent being mediocre rather than actually failing. Only three of the upper middle class boys, and none of the upper middle class girls, had grade averages below C (See Table 46, marginals). Consequently the identity crisis is not precipitated by dramatic and unarguable failure. Upper middle class parents' own experience of late occupational choice may permit them to delay their pressure for a final decision. Finally, their ability to delay and moderate their pressure on the adolescent may be dependent on a greater sophistication about the educational process. Having been in school longer than lower middle class or working class parents, and being less likely to be awed by the judgments of algebra teachers, they may be able to select for their children an anxiety level nearer to the optimum,[8] an anxiety level that helps the children succeed rather than pushing them into rebellion.

In summary, we cannot definitely explain why the hypothesis of strain between success pressure and access to means does not work for upper middle class boys who aim for lower than professional positions in the labor market. But the behavior of lower middle class boys compared to working class boys does support the hypothesis, so we are left with about the same degree of confidence we had before we tried changing indicators.

There are many ways to construct alternative measures of strain. We may present one using curriculum choice and receipt of flunk notices. We may assume that students who

8. Perhaps this greater sophistication is reflected in an interesting difference in the type of pressure upper middle class parents exert on boys with non-professional images of the future. By comparing the table in Footnote 6 with Table 54, we see that 35 per cent of upper middle class boys not aiming for professional positions receive "moderate" urging. But in the lower middle class, only 23 per cent of parents are reported as "moderately urging" college planning. Lower middle class boys are nearly as likely as upper middle class boys to get strong urging for college attendance, among those who have tentatively decided not to be professionals, but considerably fewer experience the moderate urging that may be more compatible with an optimum anxiety level.

Table 54: Higher social classes, and those aiming for professional jobs, report that their parents strongly or moderately urge college planning.

| | Image of the Future | | |
Sex and Social Class	Upper Middle	Lower, Labor Market	Marriage
	Per Cent Whose Parents Urge		
Girls			
Upper Middle	90% (21)	56% (9)	59% (32)
Lower Middle	69% (26)	64% (29)	55% (71)
Working	63% (62)	37% (132)	29% (274)
Boys			
Upper Middle	96% (23)	64% (31)	
Lower Middle	75% (44)	48% (103)	
Working	67% (98)	41% (435)	

choose college preparatory curricula are more committed to success goals than those who do not; that they have not got rid of the standards of the labor market. Receiving a flunk notice may be interpreted as the school's suggestion to these students that their aspirations are not reasonable.

On the basis of the simple articulation theory developed in Chapter 3, students choosing college preparatory curricula should be less rebellious than other students. Even among those who have received flunk notices, those with better articulation of the present with the future should be less rebellious.

From the analysis above, on the contrary, we would expect that commitment to occupational success as indicated by choosing college preparatory curricula would increase the punishing nature of flunk notices. And it should do this more strongly among boys than among girls, because boys cannot make an anticipatory substitution of marriage as a way out. The tabulation of percentage rebellious, by type

Table 55: Middle class girls, if not oriented to becoming professionals, are more likely to be oriented to becoming housewives than are working class girls.

Social Class	Of Girls Without Professional Images, Per Cent Oriented to Marriage
Upper Middle	77% (41)
Lower Middle	71% (100)
Working	68% (406)

of flunk notice received and curriculum interest, is presented in Table 56.

We see first that the receipt of college preparatory flunk notices is a much more important determinant of rebellion among boys than among girls, as expected from the analysis. Further, among girls the percentage rebellious is smaller among college preparatory students than among others, whether or not girls have received flunk notices. That is, for girls all the figures on the left are smaller than the figures

Table 56: Having received flunk notices greatly encourages rebellion among boys, especially boys with college preparatory curriculum interests.

Sex and Types of Flunk Notice Received	Curriculum Interest	
	College Preparatory	All Others
	Per Cent Rebellious	
Girls		
No Flunk Notices	11% (190)	24% (308)
College Prep Notices	19% (21)	23% (35)
Other Notices Only	40% (10)	43% (89)
Boys		
No Flunk Notices	21% (180)	37% (201)
College Prep Notices	60% (42)	54% (104)
Other Notices Only	57% (14)	63% (182)

on the right. Among boys, however, the proportion rebellious among those receiving flunk notices in college preparatory classes is slightly greater among those who remain committed to college preparatory curricula. Among boys who have received college preparatory flunk notices, 60 per cent of college preparatory boys, but only 54 per cent of others, have been rebellious. Though this difference is small, it supports the structured anomie hypothesis and contradicts the simple articulation hypothesis.[9]

Nevertheless, we cannot help being discouraged by such small differences in the above table, and by the ease with which a change in measures of success (e.g., image of the future rather than grade averages) produces results requiring *ad hoc* hypotheses. We derive similarly small and erratic results with other possible indicators of strain, not reported here.[10] Almost always there were some results that could be tentatively interpreted as supporting the hypothesis, provided enough *ad hoc* assumptions and interpretations were made.

◆

WHY IS THE EVIDENCE SO ERRATIC?

It is my conviction that one of the reasons the results of the analysis are so erratic and undependable is that the measures of strain are not independent of the consequences of the strain. For instance, if adherence to goals is punishing because of failure to achieve them, the quality of

9. It may be significant that while there were only six boys who remained committed to the college preparatory curriculum after having received *both* college preparatory *and* other flunk notices, five of them (83 per cent) had been sent out of class, and four of these five had also skipped school with a gang of kids. Four of the boys placed in this anomalous situation were from the middle class.
10. Among those tried were: aspiration higher than expectation, having taken algebra as freshman mathematics combined with a non-college curriculum choice at the time of the survey, parental pressure and curriculum choice, parental pressure combined with attachment to parents (derived from the rank of "Pleasing Parents" among four items), and low grades.

adherence to goals is likely to become so subtle and variable from time to time that a gross survey instrument of the sort we have used cannot locate it. Or our gross measures of success and failure may be contaminated by motivated perceptual distortion. Students can defensively define relative failure as moral victory to an extent sufficient to deceive a survey instrument. When both failure and success are symbolic, as they are in school, particularly, redefinition is quite easy.

A clear source of pressure which cannot be much affected by the psychological processes of the reaction formation, such as social class, may work well. Clear failure, such as below-average grades, in combination with clear pressure, may enable us to locate sources of strain with relative precision. But direct questions on symbolic loyalties and on the symbolic meaning of failure are too contaminated by the dependent variable to work well.

Perhaps a surer command of the details of the reaction formation — a good phenomenology of the psychological processes in middle class academic failures — would provide good indicators of strain. This was not available to me before making the survey, either from my own observation or from the literature I could find.

In order to be sure whether the investigation of this phenomenology would be worthwhile, we need to consider whether alternative mechanisms can account for the relations established in previous sections. If other theories are sufficient, then a weak one like the structured anomie theory is inadequate, and even the limited support we have managed to marshal for this theory takes on an importance out of proportion to its solidity.

◆

ALTERNATIVE MECHANISMS

In the following pages we will present briefly and try to refute alternative theories. If other theories are either not true, or not sufficient to account for the facts, then the structured anomie hypothesis deserves further investigation. If some other extant theory is sufficient, then there is no sense in further work on reaction formations. We first recall the evidence that led to the rejection of the theory that social classes differentially teach rebellion. Second, we will deal with the theory that the sexes are socialized differently in a way that explains the rebellion of boys. A more flexible theory, that accounts for much of the data, is the theory of peer culture. Perhaps rebellious peer culture is not primarily a response to the school, but rather is learned in the community at large. But this theory, too, seems to be inadequate to explain the data.

To begin, it may be useful to discuss briefly whether the direction of causal relationship is not the other way around, that is, whether rebellion causes failure. This was, in fact, assumed in Chapter 2, when we used failure as an element in an index of rebellion. Certainly the greater rebelliousness of boys is the chief explanation of their lower average grades. Probably even the lower scores of boys on I.Q. tests during high school is a reflection of boys' greater rebelliousness.

Failure, then, tends to be a self-confirming process among boys: failure leads to rebelliousness which leads to more dramatic and irrevocable failure. Among girls, who are not so much hurt by failure, rebelliousness is not as great, hence failure not so dramatic. The self-confirming character of failure in a status system, salient to the man who fails, is well illustrated in Arthur Miller's *Death of a Salesman*. Textbooks on salesmanship support Miller; they emphasize that in order to succeed, a man must convince himself that he is successful.

This self-confirming quality of failure (and of success) is no objection to the argument here. Only if rebelliousness *produced exclusively by factors other than failure* caused the low performance of rebels, would the argument be damaged. This alternative explanation for the association of failure and rebellion is examined below.

◆

(1) THE HYPOTHESIS OF
SOCIAL CLASS CULTURE

Social classes socialize children differently, which according to the theory encourages the adolescents to be less amenable to the social control exercised by the school. This is supported by the fact that students from higher social classes do work harder and achieve better in school, and by parental support for school activity indicated by parental urging of college education. The failure of the school's social control to govern working class children results not only in lack of achievement (apathetic response), but also in behavioral rebellion and expressive alienation, according to the theory. To this alternative, we may make the following objections.

Objection A. Although students from the working class in the sample do achieve less, they do not have higher rates of rebellion than lower middle class students. This contradicts the hypothesis, and led to the alternative hypothesis formulated in this chapter. See Chapter 4 for the relevant tabulations.

Objection B. The hypothesis fails to explain the *reversal* of the relation between social class and rebellion among boys, in the subgroup of those who fail in school. Not only is there no statistical relation between social class and rebellion in the town, but in some groups of students higher social class leads to *more* rebellion. This is in flat contradiction to such theories of rebellion as that of Hollingshead in *Elmtown's Youth.*[1]

Objection C. The hypothesis fails to explain one of the largest differences in rebelliousness, namely the sex-difference.

---

1. *Op. cit.*

◆

(2) THE HYPOTHESIS OF SEX-DIFFERENCES IN SOCIALIZATION

In order to explain the sex-differences, we might advance the hypothesis that girls, in preparation for their subordinate adult roles, are socialized to accept authority more easily than are boys.

The first objection is that the hypothesis does not explain the variation among subgroups of girls, and particularly does not explain the reduction of sex-differences when articulation of current activity with future status is controlled. The subgroups most socialized to the typically feminine role of housewife are the *most* rebellious, not the least.

This may be dealt with fairly simply. We may assume that one of the things girls accept from authorities is the image of their future status and its worth. Thus those girls most completely oriented to marriage are actually *least* properly socialized for feminine subordination. If they were properly socialized, they would subordinate their images of the future to school authority, and would submit to school authority in classes.

Objection A. But we presented evidence above (see Table 46) that girls in all but one achievement and social class sub-groups are less likely to decide to go to college, and are more likely to decide not to go. This means that they do not in fact accept the images of the future offered by authority figures as much as boys do. It is inconsistent to assume that they more readily accept labor market images but less readily accept the attendant college decisions.

Objection B. If girls accept authority more, then they should be more willing than boys to have authorities make demands that go beyond the principles of legitimacy of those authorities. For instance, they should be more willing to have authorities in school give rewards and punishments to students for characteristics irrelevant to intellectual achievement. Two questions in the schedule allow us to check this derivation.

In Table 57 the sex distribution of responses to the statement "Teachers should give good grades for neatness on themes and assignments, as well as knowledge of the subject."

Table 57: Girls are slightly more likely to agree that they should be graded for neatness than are boys.

| | Sex | |
Response	Girls	Boys
Strongly Agree	24%	25%
Agree	53%	39%
Indifferent	11%	17%
Disagree	7%	12%
Strongly Disagree	3%	3%
Don't Know	2%	3%
No Answer	0*	1%
Number	668	751

*Less than 0.5%.

Though the percentages giving the extreme responses ("Strongly Agree" and "Strongly Disagree") do not support the hypothesis that girls are more likely to accept authority, the distribution of moderate responses does support it. That is, a total of 77 per cent of the girls, but only 64 per cent of the boys agree with the statement. Conversely, a total of 10 per cent of the girls, and 15 per cent of the boys, are not willing to have intellectually irrelevant neatness criteria applied in grading. The alternative hypothesis is strengthened and the structural anomie hypothesis weakened by this relation.

But an item with a different cutting point gives the opposite relation. Responses to the statement, "Teachers have a right to expect cleanliness and neatness in dress, and should enforce this by basing grades partly on personal neatness," are reported in Table 58. It will be noted that girls are slightly *less* likely to grant teachers the right to grade them on their clothes, and are more likely to disagree with the statement, than are boys.

This relation tends to contradict the hypothesis that girls are more likely to respond favorably to authority in general. The weakness of the first relation, and the reversal of the second, is all the more surprising when we remember that boys are more rebellious than girls. And since boys are strikingly more rebellious in the classroom, we would expect them to disagree with the statements above much more than girls.

We do not argue that girls are not more responsive to authority by virtue of different personality structures,[2] but we do try to show that this is insufficient as an explanation for rebellion in high school.

In summary, the hypothesis of differential sex socialization is not sufficient as it stands to explain the differences among the subgroups of girls. We can add a hypothesis that among the things to which girls respond favorably are the images of the future held out by authority figures. This would explain the variations among subgroups of girls. But this leads to results that are either not supported or are falsified by the data. This interpretation would entail that the personalities of girls fully oriented to marriage were more similar to boys' personalities than girls oriented to the labor

2. Girls seem to be more responsive to group pressures in the Asch experiments, where the group is in league with the experimenter to mis-report their perception of the length of lines. Girls tend to be more swayed by the groups' statements, and less able to believe their own perceptions independently. See Richard S. Crutchfield, "Conformity and Character," *American Psychologist*, Vol. 10 (May 1955), pp. 191-198. Also, girls are less able to analyze a perception of a field into its components, being more confused by embedded figures, by tipped rooms, and the like. These results of perception experiments seem to show that girls are more responsive to cues present in a situation and less autonomous; among cues, of course, are authoritative cues.

Table 58: Girls are slightly *less* likely to agree that they should be graded on their dress than are boys.

Response	Sex	
	Girls	Boys
Strongly Agree	10%	12%
Agree	22%	23%
Indifferent	13%	15%
Disagree	32%	25%
Strongly Disagree	19%	21%
Don't Know	4%	3%
No Answer	1%	1%
Number	**668**	**751**

market. This cannot be disproved with our data, but it does seem a little paradoxical. Second, differential response to authority would imply a greater tendency of girls to set themselves goals of going to college, which are highly valued by the authorities of the high school. But they do not; rather they do the reverse. Third, this interpretation leads us to expect that girls would be more willing than boys to have teachers add standards of judgment to those legitimatized by the institutional purpose of learning. But the differences on the relevant items are not very large, and one of them supports, one tends to refute, the necessary hypothesis.

◈

(3) THE HYPOTHESIS OF AN EXTERNALLY
DETERMINED PEER CULTURE

A third possible alternative mechanism is externally determined peer culture. Perhaps the rebellious quality of peer culture is prescribed by the society at large, rather than determined by the status problems of the boys oriented toward the working class. A theory of peer culture could be constructed to account for many of our results as follows:

First, the peer cultures that girls and boys are supposed to develop differ a good deal. In the community studied, we could suppose that the sex-division in culture would be especially great, because the great predominance of exclusively male work places in the logging industry should allow greater autonomous development to adult male culture. This would be reflected in the greater distinctiveness of adolescent male culture.[3]

Hypothetically, the peer group culture of girls supports school achievement by making fewer demands on time (taking time away from homework), by claiming fewer rights to autonomous personal decision, and by holding favorable attitudes toward legitimate authorities. Boys' peer culture, on the other hand, takes time away from homework, is more detached from the home, school, and other legitimate institutions, claims rights of personal autonomy, and supports rebellion against school authority.

We might guess that when girls date they tend to be isolated from girls' peer culture and brought into greater contact with boys' culture. At the same time, dating makes a housewife image of the future more realistic and desirable.

3. Exclusively male environments, such as the work sites of the logging and sawmill industry, tend to give rise to a culture of "masculinity" with the following common characteristics: (1) the extensive use of profanity, especially of the obscene variety; (2) a positive evaluation of casual exploitative sexual relations; (3) recreational patterns bringing men out of the home into bars, poolrooms, etc., which have more or less exclusively male clienteles; (4) detachment of the father from child-raising, with consequent isolation of men from the conservatizing influences of children; (5) flowing from these, a general cultural instability of the family, with the wife defending the "respectable, home-loving" values against the husband's "irresponsible, masculine" orientation. See especially Norman Dennis, et al., *Coal Is Our Life*, pp. 141-162 and 212-220 (all of Chapter 5, pp. 171-245 is relevant). Also William F. Whyte, "A Slum Sex Code," *American Journal of Sociology*, Vol. 49 (July 1943), pp. 24-31; Henry Elkin, "Agressive and Erotic Tendencies in Army Life," *American Journal of Sociology*, Vol. 51 (March 1946), pp. 408-413; Katherine Archibald, *Wartime Shipyard* (Berkeley: University of California Press, 1947), pp. 15-39; Norman S. Hayner, "Taming the Lumberjack," *American Sociological Review*, Vol. 10 (April 1945), pp. 217-225.

This explains the association of girls' images of the future with rebellion, by making clear why girls aspiring to be housewives are more rebellious. Because of the greater rebellion and because of the claims made on time by dating, they achieve less in school, which explains the association of marriage market images of the future with school achievement.

Among boys, those who are poorly adjusted to peer groups, isolated from peer groups by ambitious parents, or seduced out of peer loyalties by consistently rewarding school experience, tend to lose their "natural" loyalty to peer groups. Hence under these conditions they achieve better, delay gratifications which could be obtained by participation in peer culture, and form images of their future in the professional sector of the labor market. This explains the association between images of the future and rebellion among boys.

Further, boys from the middle class who are *not* successfully isolated from peer group culture may tend to become its leaders, because they have more money, more time away from a job, and perhaps more ability and poise. As we know from small group studies, the leaders of a group often represent more fully than ordinary members the values of the group. Since in adolescent male culture these values are rebellious, the most rebellious participants in peer group culture are those originally from the middle class.[4]

Such a theory can generate most of the results found; again we must challenge the adequacy of the theory, not its truth.

Objection A. The process of "seduction" out of male peer group culture still depends on articulation of school activity with an image of a personal future status. It is the occupational meaning of the school rewards that motivates ambitious parents to isolate their children from the peer culture.

4. This would be analogous to the proposition suggested by Michels, that the socialist leaders from middle class origins are the least corruptible.

Further, boys who have accepted the school's culture to the extent of setting themselves high aspirations, but who expect to hold jobs with low prestige, are just as rebellious as boys who do not aspire higher. Finally, ambitious boys who aim for jobs not allocated by the school (in the business sector of the lower middle class) are just as rebellious as boys headed for the working class.[5]

So the explanation that boys aiming for the middle class assimilate middle class delayed-gratification patterns, which seduces them out of peer culture, is inadequate. It is necessary to add that *delayed gratification only has meaning when current activity in school is clearly connected with future status,* and when this status appears achievable. For if all ambition resulted in delay of gratification, then boys destined for the lower middle class would delay gratifications, and be less rebellious. But they are not.

In further support of this point, we found in the last chapter that loyalty to the symbols of male peer culture (cigarettes, cars, and early marriage) did not fully explain rebellion; that image of the future had an independent effect.

In other words, the peer culture hypothesis does not eliminate the necessity for the image of the future hypothesis, and does not replace the requirement of analyzing the structural articulation of the high school and the labor market.

Objection B. The peer culture hypothesis does not account for the saliency of attitudes toward formal school status systems in the rebellious peer culture. If the culture is merely absorbed from adult male working class culture, it is unusual that it should be heavily focussed on negative attitudes toward teacher fairness, toward clique domination of the student community, and the like.

Further, it is difficult to account by this hypothesis for the variability in the relation between status alienation and

5.   This tabulation is not presented here.

rebellion. We found in Chapters 2 and 4 that, among boys, alienation from the formal status system was most closely related to rebellion. Among girls, on the other hand, alienation from the informal systems was more closely related to rebellion.

Finally, the incapacity of the most rebellious sex, boys (especially from the middle class), to decide not to succeed is difficult to explain by any hypothesis that designates them the fullest participants in a culture originally alien from the school. It would seem that if lower middle class boys become leaders in a rebellious subculture, they would then reject the success goals held out by the formal system *more* violently. Since they reject them less violently, we are almost forced to believe that their participation in the rebellious culture helps rid them of their high school's standards of success. The rebelliousness serves a function of permitting school standards to be rejected, and part of the adherence to rebellious culture must be motivated by this function.

Objection C. The peer group culture hypothesis does not explain the greater rebelliousness of girls who lower their labor market expectations without substituting an image of their future in the marriage market. There was evidence that these girls come from the most conforming subgroup of girls, those oriented to the high positions in the labor market. They do not show signs of long standing alienation, such as behavioral rebellion and negativism, which indicates that they have probably been conformists in the past. Even though they belong to the most conforming subculture, and have not been exposed to the rebellious subculture of boys through dating, they are rebellious on the indicators not requiring long-standing alienation. Their alienation is explained by the mechanism offered above, but not by the mechanisms of peer culture transmission.

In summary, the peer culture hypothesis is insufficient to explain which students are seducible by the school. This requires the addition of the articulation analysis. It does not explain the content of rebellious culture, particularly the evidence of internalization of school goals among the most rebellious subgroups. Nor does it explain the content of alienation from the school status systems on which students have staked their self-respect, analyzed in Chapter 4. Finally, it does not explain the appearance of alienated attitudes and behavior in subgroups apparently isolated from the peer culture.

In short, the peer culture hypothesis does not explain the differential motivation to give loyalty to an alienated peer culture, nor the motivation to bring alienated values into peer relations.

◆

CONCLUSION

Even though the mechanism of strain between internalized standards of success and inaccessibility of the means producing rebellion seems uncomfortably fragile under the impact of changing indicators, there are some results which are difficult to explain on any other hypothesis. Boys more than girls, and middle class boys more than working class boys, have internalized the standards of universalistic achievement as a standard of self-evaluation. Even when confronted with academic failure, boys, and particularly middle class boys, refuse to abandon the possibility of college, and among the academically unsuccessful, boys, particularly middle class boys, are the most rebellious.

Some of the deviations from this pattern may be due to the fact that the means of success allocated by the school are symbolic means — guarantees of future status. Perhaps our indicators of failure are not convincing signs of failure among some subgroups.

The hypothesis of sex-differences in attitudes to authority in general could not explain the relations between images of the future and rebellion within the sexes. When modified to allow this, the hypothesis led to the derivation of results that were not verified. Girls proved little or no more willing than boys to accept extensions of their "zone of indifference" into matters of personal neatness, and less likely than boys to have an image of the future that would elicit the highest evaluation from school authorities.

The hypothesis of exogenously determined peer culture creating rebellion failed to explain the association of loyalty to itself with images of the future, nor did it explain why the image of the future had an effect independent of loyalty to the typical symbols of peer culture. It also failed to explain the saliency of goals of educational achievement, and the saliency of rejection of school status systems, in the culture of rebellious students. Finally, it was unable to explain how one of the groups we would expect to be most isolated from the influences of the male rebellious peer group came to have great attitudinal similarity to it.

We are left with the necessity to accept tentatively the delicate and elusive mechanism of status deprivation and structured anomie. One of the first tasks confronting future research is to grasp firmly the phenomenology of the hypothesized reaction formation. This might be accomplished by locating middle class failures through survey instruments or school records, and intensive clinical-type interviewing which might provide indicators delicate enough to isolate consequences and sources of the strain, and defense mechanisms against the strain.

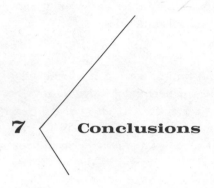

7   Conclusions

"Nor do I recommend the way into the sands of whirling facts which blow into the eyes and ears until nothing can be seen and heard." — T. H. Marshall

We have shown that a good deal of rebellion is associated with a complex set of emotions and attitudes which we called "expressive alienation." Some rebellion is not caused by this set of emotions and attitudes, but rather by random situational factors, the behavior of teachers provoking rebellion, and so forth. Insofar as rebellion is a manifestation of the psychological state of expressive alienation, we have a theory of it here. Insofar as rebellion is caused by teacher behavior and accidents of social interaction, we do not have a theory of it. Thus the first causal link that we tried to establish (in Chapter 2) was that rebellious behavior was in part an expression of a set of attitudes and emotions, as diagrammed in Figure 1.

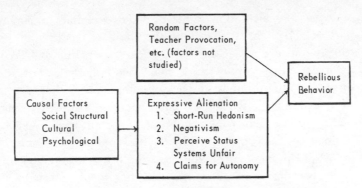

Figure 1: The Relation Between Expressive Alienation and Rebellion

The evidence showed that rebellion is a manifestation of expressive alienation, being strongly and consistently related to the attitudes of expressive alienation. These attitudes, which we derived from Albert Cohen's description of the delinquent subculture and Redl and Wineman's descriptions of defective ego-functioning,[1] were: short-run hedonism, whether measured in its emotional, cognitive, or motivational aspects; negativism, or the negative evaluation of conformity and conformists as such; perception of the status systems of the school as unfair, and particularly seeing the status systems administered by school authorities as unfair; and claims to autonomy from adult interference, especially objecting to adult interference with smoking and car-owning rights. The fact that these attitudes were independently ascribed to delinquents by scholars operating with quite different conceptual schemes is already substantial evidence. But the strong relations between these attitudes and rebellious behavior, established in Chapter 2, definitely show the causal connection between these attitudes and non-conformity.

This means that, if we can invent and establish a theory

1.   Albert K. Cohen, *Delinquent Boys, op. cit.;* Fritz Redl and David Wineman, *Children Who Hate, loc. cit.*

of expressive alienation, we will have explained a major part of rebellion. The rest of the book is an attempt to specify and document the "causal factors" in Figure 1. We dealt with these under three main headings: social structural, of which the most important component is the degree of articulation between high school curricula and the labor market; cultural, of which the most important component is the degree of acceptance of the doctrine of adolescent inferiority; and psychological, the most important component of which is exposure to failure when one has deeply internalized success norms.

Chapters 3 and 4 were devoted to elaborating the social-structural causes of expressive alienation, and hence of rebellious behavior. We first showed that the statistics on the distribution of official juvenile delinquency, plus qualitative information of various kinds, suggested the following summary hypothesis: Expressive alienation appears to be most common among *the adolescents of school age* who are exposed to *more universalistic labor markets* and who *will fill* the manual working class positions in those markets. The groups expected to have high delinquency rates according to this specification are urban working class males of high school age, especially if they have low intelligence, or live in slums, or are members of depressed ethnic minorities. The detailed argument for this summary of previously established correlations is found in Chapter 3.

In order to explain this general presumed "fact" of the distribution of expressive alienation, we showed, first, that the group described in the hypothesis had poor articulation between their school activity and their futures, and second, that other groups (smaller in size) among girls who had poor articulation also were rebellious. We further showed that poor articulation *did not* explain that part of rebellion which was not a manifestation of expressive alienation, and that the articulation theory was better than the social-class socialization theory in predicting rebellion. In fact, the social class socialization theory of rebellion is flatly contradicted by the data, since there are groups of males in which the higher social classes have higher rates of rebellion.

The end result of this analysis was to elaborate the diagram of the causal structure in one particular part, illustrated in Figure 2. As seen from the diagram, we gave evidence in Chapters 3 and 4 that a wide variety of variables that are known to be associated with delinquencies are theoretically reducible to a single variable: the degree of articulation of present activity with future status. And with the use of this concept we located rebellious groups of girls, much smaller than the group of working class oriented boys. The theoretical importance of this is much different from merely adding another variable to the prediction of delinquency. It shows that the theoretical concept of poor articulation *predicts the variables* that will be related to rebellion. This is, of course, the function of a theory, to predict *the relations among* naturally occurring phenomena, not to predict the phenomena themselves.[2]

Then in Chapter 5 we discussed the cultural sources of expressive alienation, arguing that the lack of articulation between present activity and future status produced *ritual poverty* among the future workers. That is, they had few symbols, none provided by the school, to render their activity meaningful in terms of the central problem of adolescence: growing up. In their search for symbols to render

2.   Confusion on this score is the source of a great many difficulties in discussions of prediction, projection, prophecy, and theory. One predicts phenomena from other phenomena, and can only do so after the other phenomena have occurred. One projects phenomena by *guessing* at the future of predictors (e.g., by guessing the future birthrate in population projections). One prophesies by guessing at the future of the phenomena of interest. One theorizes by specifying in some systematic way which variables will be predictors. This confusion, aside from tempting sociologists to make stupid, but unimportant, mistakes in the philosophy of science, has confused the substantive discusssion especially of Marxian thought. Marx's theories, and most of his projections, are largely true. Only his prophecies failed. But this is a topic for a different place.

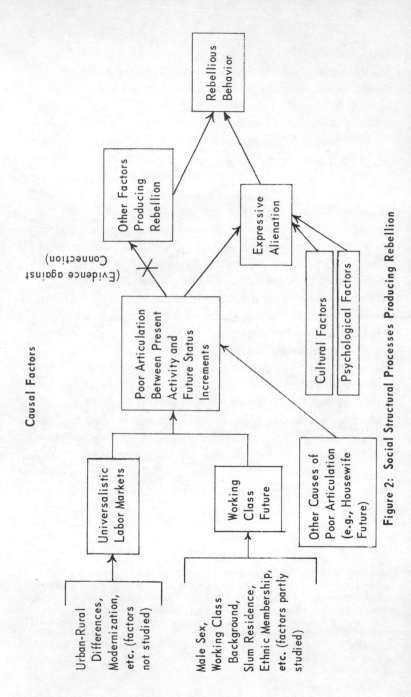

174

Figure 2: Social Structural Processes Producing Rebellion

the school experience meaningful, poorly articulated adolescents chose symbols of growing up which claimed adult rights while they were still adolescents. These claims were particularly prevalent among boys, whose problem of how to become adult is a more acute, active one. Then we showed that this rejection by adolescents of the doctrine of the rightlessness of adolescents was closely related to rebellion. This produced a different elaboration of the causal picture, illustrated in Figure 3.

In Chapter 6 we turned to the problem of trying to demonstrate the "reaction formation" theory of rebellion, the theory that one does not rebel emotionally against standards which have not been internalized. This theory was developed in the area of delinquency primarily by Robert K. Merton.[3] Briefly we tried to show that *among failures, those most subject to success pressure were most expressively alienated and most rebellious.* First, we showed that success pressure was greater on boys, and greater in the middle class. Then we showed that rates of rebellion *among failures* in school were higher among boy failures and higher among middle class failures. Several indirect tests of this theory were carried out, but the theory encountered substantial difficulties. However, the difficulties seem to be nowhere near as serious as the problems with various socialization or peer group culture theories. The details of this argument are presented in Chapter 6. We concluded, then, for want of a better explanation of the data, and the clear inadequacy of the main alternative theories, that the psychological mechanism producing rebellion is largely the reaction-formation. The inferred causal structure is diagrammed in Figure 4.

The location and documentation of the causal structures diagrammed in Figures 1 through 4 is the intellectual purpose of this book. Although they may appear sufficiently complicated, the reader who has been following the argu-

3.   Robert K. Merton, "Social Structure and Anomie," *loc. cit.*

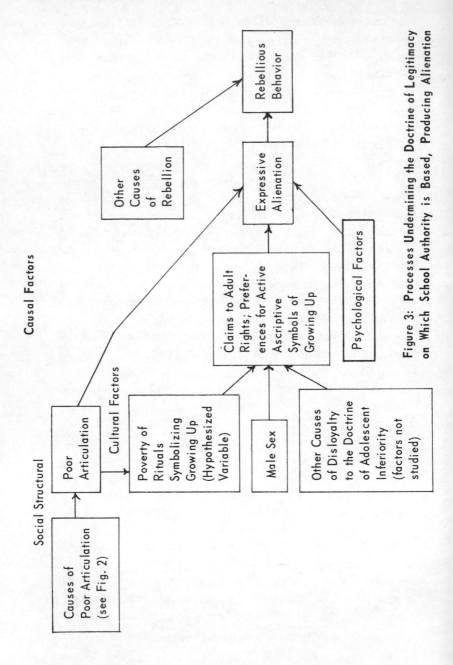

Causal Factors

Social Structural

Cultural Factors

Causes of Poor Articulation (see Fig. 2)

Poor Articulation

Poverty of Rituals Symbolizing Growing Up (Hypothesized Variable)

Claims to Adult Rights; Preferences for Active Ascriptive Symbols of Growing Up

Male Sex

Other Causes of Disloyalty to the Doctrine of Adolescent Inferiority (factors not studied)

Psychological Factors

Other Causes of Rebellion

Expressive Alienation

Rebellious Behavior

Figure 3: Processes Undermining the Doctrine of Legitimacy on Which School Authority is Based, Producing Alienation

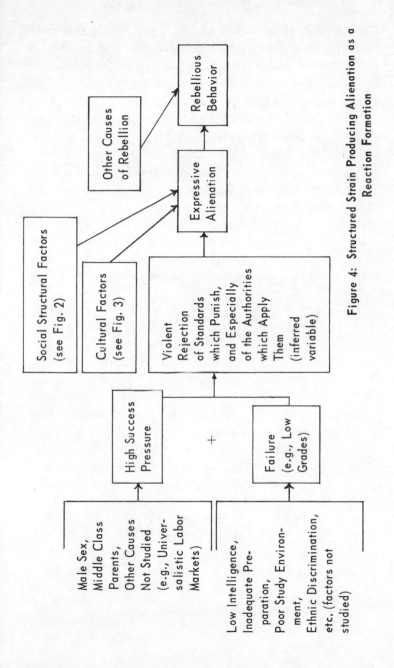

Figure 4: Structured Strain Producing Alienation as a Reaction Formation

ment through all its statistical details will testify that these diagrams are a great deal less complicated than the data on which they are based. The object of science is to complicate the theory just enough to reduce the complication of the data. This seems to have been accomplished.

In order to be useful scientifically, a theory must go beyond the data which have suggested it. I collected the data with the idea that they would verify the theory advanced in Figures 1 through 4. With occasional failures and difficulties, I think they have. But any evidence from any social environment showing that expressive alienation (and deviant behavior insofar as it is a manifestation of expressive alienation) is not due to these causes, is contrary or contradictory to the theory advanced here. In short, such evidence would show that I am wrong. I expect to be partly wrong.

◆

WHAT IS TO BE DONE?

This leaves us then with the question of what to do about it? In the first place, it is not clear that anything needs to be done, in a fundamental sense. The rebellion we talk about is basically an inconvenience to teachers and school administrators. Reasonably competent teaching and administration can exercise situational control, so that education may proceed. This means that some teachers will need to be fired for not being able to maintain classroom control, but most such teachers seem to me to be also ineffective educators at the high school level, and their elimination may be a good thing.[4] The main reasons for worrying about what is to be done are the unhappiness of adolescents whose adolescence is meaningless, and the possibil-

4. The reason for the correlation between disciplinary capacity and educational effectiveness is that dramatic sense — a sense of timing and a capacity to gauge audience response — is a prime tool of classroom control, and also a prime tool for focusing attention for educational purposes.

ity that expressively alienated students will find themselves in more serious trouble and go to prison.

Even given these costs, we must of course weigh the costs of alternatives. For instance, it has been clear to students of the question for considerable time that a large part of the higher delinquency rate of Negro youth is due to employment discrimination against Negro adult males. This discrimination has the double effect of destroying hope among Negro adolescents and of making the Negro family continually mother-centered, and hence weak. Clearly the society has "decided" that reducing Negro delinquency is not worth the cost of having to reduce discrimination in employment. Whether employment discrimination is valuable enough to be worth its costs in terms of delinquency is not, of course, a scientific question.

The major practical conclusion of the analysis above is that rebellious behavior is largely a reaction to the school itself and to its promises, not a failure of the family or community. High school students can be motivated to conform by paying them in the realistic coin of future adult advantages. Except perhaps for pathological cases, any students can be motivated to conform if the school can realistically promise something valuable to them as a reward for working hard. But for a large part of the population, especially the adolescents who will enter the male working class or the female candidates for early marriage, the school has nothing to promise.

This means that the problem of order in schools, of juvenile delinquency and expressive alienation, is not easy to solve. *For the reason that the school cannot promise much is that the society cannot promise much.* Tinkering a bit with the curriculum to "make it more meaningful" for duller children will have little effect. Culture is "meaningful" for the average man as it relates to something he wants to do. A high school student wants to grow up into an adult who is successful by adult standards. Culture that is not relevant to the problem of growing up successful, however useful it may be for citizens or householders, will not make school meaningful.

What are the possible courses of action that might lead to a worthwhile adolescence for those who will fill the ranks of the working class? The first requisite is a far more definite arrangement between the people who will hire manual labor and the schools which train it. Any increased labor market rights — increased chances of jobs, increased pay, advanced standing in apprenticeship programs, etc. — will tend to render vocational training meaningful. At present, except in a very few schools in large cities, vocational training is a farce. It serves the function of a "liberal arts" preparation for living in the working class, but not the function of providing saleable skills. In fact, the dollars-and-cents economic value of Latin to the student is probably higher than the value of any vocational courses, except secretarial courses for girls.

The great difficulty is that employers of manual labor do not know what they need — or perhaps do not need anything in particular. Is there anything that a high school can teach which employers of manual labor would be willing to pay for, if it were learned well? In general, the answer is no. Neither physical abilities nor reliability, the two main variables of interest to employers of manual labor, are much influenced by schooling. Employers concerned with securing reliable workers may require high school diplomas as evidence of good discipline. Otherwise they can train workers better and cheaper than a high school can, on the job.

Although this is the general situation, there are a few cases in which connections can be made between school and jobs. Each increase in such connections should increase the meaningfulness of school for future workers, who create most of the trouble.

A second requirement is to extend secretarial training to boys who will not go on to college. Manual jobs are becoming scarcer, while the bureaucratic sector of the labor market is still expanding almost as fast as the professional sector. Insofar as vocational training for boys now is not a farce, it is preparing them for jobs which will not exist in the near future.

More fundamental experiments with the structure of careers in the whole society, so that jobs could become part of a real life-plan for the majority of workers, are apparently beyond our knowledge and power at the present time. If exact knowledge of what each man had to do to better his condition were available to him, and if it were guaranteed to each that by doing it he would improve his situation, much of the meaninglessness of work, and of education for work, would disappear. But this would entail a different society from the one we have now, a society of secure employment, with a predictable future of labor market demand, with precise information on where each man stands now and what he is capable of, and mechanisms by which opportunities in the labor market are offered to those, and only those, whose abilities it will stretch to get them. We are now closer to being technically able to construct the world of work this way than we ever have been before. But a society not yet capable of eliminating gross and obvious racial employment discrimination ought to be cautious about adopting utopian schemes to give exactly the right job to the right man.

The second point at which attention might be directed is the doctrine of adolescent inferiority. The doctrine that teachers are superior to students, and that students ought to imitate them in certain respects (especially in knowledge and competence), is necessary for systematic education. It is the justification for the teacher telling the student what to study. But in practically all societies, the doctrine of the inferiority of students is closely intertwined with the doctrine of the inferiority of the young. As we have seen, when students do not consider that the young are and ought to be inferior, they encounter trouble with the authority system. Among boys, particularly, the degree of acceptance of the doctrine that adolescents ought not to have adult rights is very closely related to rebellion.

The Puritanism of the traditional "official" culture of the United States makes it difficult to discuss rationally exactly when and how adolescents should be introduced to the adult rights of sex, tobacco, alcohol, high powered cars, and spending their own money as they please. Though most adults treat these things as the good things in life, they do not allow official representatives of the culture to say that these are the good things. It is this official hypocrisy that is behind the famous definition of a teacher as a man hired to tell lies to little boys. Even in the most Puritan cultures, purity is confined to a select minority, while most adults happily live out their unrespectable lives. Somehow children must avoid becoming like they are told to become in school, in order to become like adults. Rebellion, particularly for boys, is a nearly inevitable result of the two-faced character of ideals of adulthood. And, as we saw, boys do in fact claim many more of the rights of men, while still boys, than girls do.

It is not the province of a sociologist to say whether it is better for adults to become Puritans, or for school officials to defend our ideals of adulthood as they actually exist — sex, high-powered cars, liquor, and all — or to continue the hypocrisy. It seems likely that for some time we will continue with hypocrisy, with the strain between official and unofficial versions of what it means to be an adult. But it seems likely that we will decrease the stridency in our official Puritanism. Our focus here is on the side effects of this cultural strain, as students' objection to the doctrine of adolescent inferiority creates problems of authority in the high school.

This challenge to the doctrine is partly motivated merely by rebellion against the career meaninglessness of the school, as we showed above. But it is also clear that lack of belief in the inferiority and lesser rights of youth has an independent effect on rebellion. One of the most interesting questions emerging from the results here is the problem of how people learn what is appropriate for adolescents and what it means to be an adult. People vary a great deal, apparently, in their beliefs about age and its proper relation to behavior, and these variations cause striking variations in rebellion, in whether students participate primarily in the asexual official teen culture or in the proto-sexual dating teen culture, in how they think about military life, in their ratings of the importance of parents as opposed to peers in their behavior, and many other important things. We are almost as ignorant of how people learn or fail to learn to act their age as we are of how they learn to be men or women. These are the factors described as "not studied" in Figure 3. Reference to several of the tables in Chapter 5 will show that a large part of the variation in age-grading beliefs is due to these "other factors."

Thus it might be possible to control much of the rebellion of high school students if one could teach "boys" to be boys instead of men. They really are men, as strong and as intelligent as other men, by the end of high school. False doctrines of inferiority have worked before to shore up authority systems, however, and presumably this one can be made to work better. Again, the worth of it is not a scientific question.

The psychological strain which produces the reaction formation may also be capable of reduction. If it does, indeed, turn out that the upper-middle class family has techniques for keeping the anxiety level near the optimum, for adjusting the amount of pressure to succeed to the ability of the child, the techniques of this adjustment could be studied. Some of these techniques might be of the kind that can be applied directly by the school to reduce the bitterness of failing students. And part of the techniques might be capable of being transmitted to lower-middle class and working class mothers and fathers, both through the school and through popular magazines.

Before this can be done, it is necessary to know a great deal more about the exact conditions under which failure hurts most, and how to relieve the hurt. It is one of the costs of equality of opportunity that people have no one to blame for their failures, and it is one of the comforts of holding securely an inferior position, as a woman for instance, that one need never fail. But exactly how much the failure entailed in equality has to hurt, and what salves to wounded egos are effective in relieving the pain if not in curing the failure, are topics well worth investigating.

There are ideological problems in studying this objectively. Men of good will, especially if they are close to adolescents, prefer to pretend that the various paths merely lead to different — but equally valuable — forms of success. This means that they have humane objections to calling failure by its name, even for purposes of investigation. The refusal to call things by their names may be one of the salves that in fact reduces the pain. I doubt that it has much effect, for I think that most adolescents do find out what is valued by society and translate this into self-judgments and judgments of each other within the school. But this deserves special investigation.

If it turns out that "failure" from the point of view of the larger society can be redefined as another path to success, this will probably have some impact on the motivational effectiveness of the system. That is, the much-discussed "wastage of talent" may be partly due to the effects of not telling adolescents clearly what the society regards as success and failure. If truck driving is defined as another kind of success, some potential nuclear physicists will prefer that kind of success. Again the worth of preventing high school expressive alienation is not a scientific question.

◆

CONCLUDING COMMENTS

One of the favorite substitutes for religion in a secular world is pontification on social problems without investigating them. Most people are qualified to talk on the problem of this book, because they have either been good adolescents or overcame their bad streak. Most have raised good adolescents. In the same way almost everyone is qualified to speak on health and disease, because they have either been well all their lives or else they have recovered health. Painstaking research into the causes of phenomena, special jargon, professional qualification, and patience to read difficult material, are no more important for social problems than for medical problems.[5] And just as every intelligent doctor should be able to write of the causes of glaucoma in a way to interest the intelligent, literate layman, so the sociologist should write crystal prose.

This book has frankly intended to be a complicated book, because the phenomenon it tries to explain is complicated. If, by this page, readers are classified into those committed enough to want to find out the causes of rebellion through further research, and those who have stopped reading before now,[6] its purpose is partly accomplished.

5. Much of the current popular literature on juvenile delinquency reminds me of the analogy to medicine at an earlier time, as illustrated for instance by Chekhov's comment on ". . .Tolstoy's stubborn brashness in treating of things he doesn't know and doesn't understand. Thus his pronouncements on syphilis, foundling homes, women's repugnance to cohabitation, and so on are not only debatable, but show him to be an ignoramus who has never taken the trouble during his long life to read two or three books written by specialists." *The Selected Letters of Anton Chekhov*, ed. by Lillian Hellman (New York: Farrar, Straus, 1955), p. 85. See also pp. 153, 156, 166. See also Claude Bernard, *Introduction to the Study of Experimental Medicine* (New York: Dover, 1957).
6. If these have happened to start with the conclusion, they might read, instead of this book, Hollingshead, *Elmtown's Youth, op. cit.* The explanation of rebellion in Elmtown is a good deal simpler than in California.

Appendix on Method

The interviewing on which the analysis was based was done by a pencil and paper schedule, a copy of which is included in Appendix II. Interview schedules were passed out to the teachers of the social science classes, which also function as "homerooms." Most of a class hour was given over to administering the questionnaire. In the mentally retarded classes, two or three class hours were used. All interview schedules were considered "usable" and were transferred to IBM cards, even if most of the responses were "No Answer" (or worse).

Administered as part of the school program by school authorities, the interview itself is a relatively close replica of the classroom situation it studies. Not obeying the implicit command to "answer the question" is, therefore, a measure of rebellion, correlated with other types of rebellion (see Table 1).

Table I: **On most items, rebels have higher non-response rates than conforming students.**

Magnitude of Differences in No Answer Rate	Number of Items Where Rebels Have More No Answers	Number of Items Where Conformers Have More No Answers
More than 3%	7	—
From 2 to 3%	3	1
From 1 to 2%	13	6
Less than 1%	13	9
Total	36	16

That is, rebels had a higher non-response rate on thirty-six of the fifty-two items that could be analyzed for non-response. This is true even though those who did not answer the questions on rebellion were classified as "conformers." Some of the other questions could not be used to compute a non-response rate, either because they were designed not to be answered by some people or because of peculiarities of the coding scheme. (A Wilcoxon matched-pairs signed-ranks test applied to the percentage differences in non-response rate between rebels and non-rebels gives a one-tailed probability of the null hypothesis of approximately 0.0005. Such a test assumes that non-response is independent among items, which is almost certainly not true.)

This association between rebellion and non-response holds, even when curriculum interest is held constant, leading us to suspect that it is not merely the lesser sophistication of rebels which accounts for their non-response (see Table II). In addition, Table II shows that non-response, like rebellion, is more common among boys than girls, and more common among those not on college preparatory curricula. The "No Answer" responses for sex and curriculum interest have been eliminated from Table II, giving fifty instead of fifty-two items.

Table II: Percentage of "No Answer" responses to 50
items, by sex, curriculum interest, and rebellion. (Numbers
in parenthesis are numbers of respondents. The base for the
percentage is this number times 50.)

| Sex[a] and Rebellion[b] | Curriculum Interest[c] | |
	College Preparatory	Other
Girls		
Well-Behaved	0.72% (196)	1.22% (314)
Rebellious	0.69% (29)	1.78% (119)
Boys		
Well-Behaved	1.06% (173)	2.30% (242)
Rebellious	1.41% (75)	2.41% (249)

a. Those who did not answer the question on sex are omitted.

b. Rebellious students either skipped with a group or were sent
    out of class. A "No Answer" response was treated as indicat-
    ing good behavior on the item to which no answer was given,
    so that any relation between rebellion and non-response would
    not be produced by a relation between non-responses on differ-
    ent items.

c. Those who did not answer the curriculum interest question are
    omitted. In the body of the book, they are included among those
    giving "ambiguous" answers. This explains the different num-
    bers of respondents here.

Boys' non-response rate is higher than girls', in each curriculum interest group and among both rebels and well-behaved. Among both boys and girls, rebellious and well-behaved, those on college preparatory curricula are more likely to answer the questions. And in three out of four cases,
rebels are more likely not to respond than well-behaved students, whatever their sex or curriculum interest. Only college
preparatory girls depart from this pattern.

The pattern of Table II, then, is essentially similar to the
pattern of some tables in Chapter 4, in which some attitude
indicating expressive alienation was shown to be related
to articulation, whether or not students had become rebel-

lious in behavior. Though in slightly different format, the essential result of Table II is that sex and curriculum interest are closely related to non-response, just as they are, for example, to short-run hedonism, whether or not the alienated attitude that non-response indicates has yet resulted in behavioral rebellion.

In other words, non-responses do not appreciably confuse the inferences drawn in the main body of the book, but rather serve as an independent test of the main hypothesis. Rebels, and those who, on theoretical grounds, we expect to be expressively alienated, do not obey the command to answer the question when it is given in a classroom-like interviewing situation, which uses the authority system of high school to secure answers.

SAMPLING PROCEDURES

The process of sampling for an exploratory study of this kind involves a number of stages:

(1) The choice of the "global" universe within which to select the sampling universes. In this case the global universe was the school. As pointed out in Chapter 1, the community and school selected differ somewhat from others; further, the community and school selected differ along dimensions known to be crucial to the problems of the investigation (for instance, it is nearly homogeneous ethnically, and it is a small town). This means that the universe to which we want to generalize is certainly different from the universe sampled.

(2) The choice of events to observe, within the global universe. Events that did not seem relevant to the investigation were more or less deliberately not seen, and not recorded.

(3) Intervention in the universe to create events of interest to the investigation. The exploratory survey and the

survey analyzed here were interventions of this kind. As demonstrated immediately above, the manner of intervention affects the response of the subjects. I intervened by making use of the teacher's authority to create events interesting to me. The nature of events created was affected by the authoritative manner of intervention. The entire material from the questionnaires consists of events that would not have existed had I not intervened, though presumably they are related to events that actually occur in the school.

Aside from the known differential response to my intervention, there were presumably differentials in likelihood of being exposed to the intervention. During the week when the main questionnaire was administered, there was a flu epidemic in the area. Consequently the number of absentees was higher than usual. Further, there was a considerable under-representation of girls among the respondents. This suggests that some social variables affected the likelihood of appearing in the sampled population.

Perhaps girls were especially likely to catch (or be incapacitated by) the flu, or perhaps they were especially likely to claim the exemptions from the student role legitimated by this physical incapacity. Or, finally, perhaps parents were more likely to honor claims for exemption by girls, since girls were less likely to have histories of truancy.

How and whether any of these possible explanations of the high loss of girls would have affected the internal comparisons, I have no way of knowing. The social dynamics of catching flu and of claiming exemption from school duties on the basis of physical incapacity are too little understood to make any firm judgment.[1] However, it seems that if social factors as gross as the ones studied above exert sufficient effect to upset the analysis, then at least some folklore would exist on the subject.

---

1. Girls generally have a higher rate of absenteeism. As far as I know, this has never been adequately explained. Presumably it has to do either with the physiology or with the social definition of menstruation.

Likewise, truants (particularly chronic truants) were very likely undersampled. But I know of no reason to suspect that the truants out of school on the sampling day would be appreciably different from former truants in school, except perhaps for more extreme rebelliousness.

Finally, sampling only within the school omits the "dropouts" among the teen-age population, which probably accounts for the relative under-representation of seniors.

All the students answered half of the exploratory survey. This was then analyzed by hand, using high school students from five U.S. History classes for one hour each and one group of students recruited from the study hall. A total of ninety-six students worked one hour tallying the survey. Since a period of about three months elapsed between this survey (which was identified by a completely different label, as having to do with accreditation) and the final one, I doubt if much influence remained. Clearly with such unskilled help, not much accuracy is to be expected. Since very few of the results of this survey are included here (one tabulation in Chapter 5), I will not discuss it in detail.

The main survey, on which the analysis in the book is based, was given to all the students present. Since it was to be used as evidence, much more care was taken to preserve the events (in code, of course) throughout the analysis. I edited the questionnaire myself. I hired the keypunching onto IBM cards. Then I tabulated the IBM cards myself. Since these procedures are fairly routine, I need only say that I am confident the events analyzed in the study are, with a very small margin of error, coded versions of the events that happened on the day the survey was given.

◆

STATISTICAL AND MEASUREMENT PROBLEMS

It has probably been noted that I have used very few significance tests and very weak measuring instruments. The explanation is fairly simple. The computational labor involved and the extensive exposition of cautions to the reader that would be necessary to make honest use of refined techniques would not, I believe, have contributed appreciably to the scientific value of the observations.

In the first place, the theoretical purposes of the study meant that we needed to generalize to a universe not efficiently sampled. The extensive peculiarities of the sample, outlined in the introduction and immediately above, meant that ordinary levels of significance were too weak. The relations of interest had to be maintained with several indicators, and fairly strongly, before they could be considered at all solid. Ordinary levels of acceptability are too lax for such a study.

Before the analysis of the data, I did construct a set of specific hypotheses and hypothetical tables, predicting the direction of the relations. These specific hypotheses were derived from the theory presented in the monograph, as far as it was developed at the time. But they also involved guesses on the meaning of various indicators (partly based on the results of the exploratory survey) and a relatively large amount of empirical intuition derived from familiarity with the school. How much theory and how much empirical intuition was involved in the construction of such hypothetical tables, I cannot tell. In this way I thought I would avoid the usual difficulty of *post hoc* hypotheses — that is, I could at least isolate the predictions from the interpretations evolved during the analysis. As the analysis proceeded, however I decided this was not the most efficient way of setting about this kind of study.

First, the tables constructed prior to the survey used single item indicators whose discriminating power was sometimes not great enough to provide aesthetically satisfying results. Even when the tests held up, I (and presumably the potential reader) was left with a feeling that the whole analysis might be confounded by peculiarities of the indicators. Second, the extensive uniqueness of the sample did not strike me forcibly until I began to write. This meant that I needed not only significance, but size and regularity, to generalize with any confidence. Third, the relatively large size of the sample meant that statistical tests would support unimportant results. Finally, some of the variables (especially sex) had such a great effect that tables previously set up for the whole sample had to be elaborated to eliminate major confounding factors. When the analyst begins changing tables around from the hypothesized tables, he is likely to over-represent (even to himself) the tables he "substantially predicted." This violates the assumptions of significance tests.

Instead, I decided on the approximate level of differences that had to show up in the tables of relations between the main variables of interest. I decided that about 30 to 40 per cent differences would be sufficient for the purposes at hand. This provided a "satisficing" criterion controlling the expenditure of resources on information gathering.[2]

Then I set about using several items from the questionnaires to create a partial ordering[3] of respondents, adding items until I began to achieve differences of the magnitude

2. See Herbert Simon, *Models of Man: Social and Rational* (New York: John Wiley, 1957), pp. 241-260, for a discussion of models of decision which take into account computational and information gathering costs. Simon does not discuss explicitly the application of this model to research decisions, but this is an easy specification of the model.

3. A partial ordering means that any particular respondent may be said to be higher or lower on the variable in question than part of the respondents, but is not ordered on the variable with respect to all respondents. For instance, the response pattern − − + is clearly "more of something" than − − −, and "less of something" than − + + or + − +. But this responsive pattern is not ordered with respect to the pattern − + − or + + −.

More formally, "A *partially ordered system* is any set P with a binary relation $\leq$ which satisfies the reflexive, anti-symmetric, and transitive laws . . ." Garrett Birkhoff and Saunders MacLane, *A Survey of Modern Algebra* (rev. ed.) (New York: MacMillan, 1953), p. 349. "Reflexive: For all X, $X \leq X$; Anti-Symmetric: If $X \leq Y$ and $Y \leq X$, then $X = Y$; Transitive: If $X \leq Y$ and $Y \leq Z$, then $X \leq Z$." *Ibid., p.* 336.

The "equals" symbol in this case denotes X having the same response pattern as Y. The "less than" symbol denotes Y having a response pattern with a positive response in every case where X has a positive response, and having at least one further positive response.

that satisfied me between the extreme cells. Ordinarily I did not go beyond this level, because the numbers in the cells became too small to give the nearly perfect sign-test patterns, which I also considered essential for economy in presentation.[4]

This procedure is extremely cheap in tabulating and computing time, an important consideration when many variables are being considered. Further, I believed at the time a simple dichotomy was generally a sufficiently precise measurement during multivariate analysis, which means that for the few tabulations where a more precise measure is needed it is not worthwhile to go beyond a partial ordering. I no longer believe this, and would design the study differently now.

A closer approach to a fully ordinal scale would be justified if one of the main purposes of the study were to provide tools needed to investigate a well-developed theoretical field. Or if the study did sample the population of interest adequately, more precise measures could be used to advance from the *establishment* of relations to the *estimation of size* of relations. Because the mathematics of estimation is so much more powerful for ordinal and cardinal measures, it might be necessary to construct better measures of the variables.

The application of a sign test or a ranked-difference in proportions test does not use the information that $X = Y$, and consequently does not depend on the assumption that X and Y are concentrated at a particular point on any underlying continuum if they have the same response pattern. Instead, it claims that on an underlying continuum (if one exists), some interval containing X and Y ($X = Y$) will be either to the left or to the right of the point Z, according as Z is "less than" or "greater than" X and Y by the above interpretation of the ordering relation.

4.   According to the procedure for partitioning the variation of a proportion used in Chapter 5, this criterion is approximately equivalent to demanding that the combination of items chosen account for from 30 to 40 per cent of the total variation. The average of the summed effects of the theoretically relevant variables (i.e., excluding sex) in Chapter 5 is about .32.

Since I have not used any fully ordinal scales nor made any inferences that depended on the ordinality of the scales, I have not computed reproducibilities or other measures of goodness of fit to more powerful measurement models. For the establishment of relations, I would argue that a partial ordering combined with appropriate tests ought to be powerful enough in large sample investigations.

For these various reasons, the model of analytical procedure followed here departs radically from the hypothesis-testing model on which most statistical methods are built.[5] Though it is, no doubt, a stochastic process whose probability of "success" is affected by the strength of the relations in the data and the number of cases, I am not competent to develop statistical procedures that would fit. Consequently, I have depended on intuitive judgments of statistical significance, trying to be cautious. By "cautious" I mean preferring, in general, to make errors of failing to find relations that actually held (commonly called "Type II Errors") to errors of finding relations that were not there.

For example, my general procedure was to include "Don't Know" and "No Answer" responses as cases tending to disprove the hypothesis in question. Except in a few cases, explicitly labeled in the text, I have left the "Don't Know" and "No Answer" responses in the base numbers. If the relation was not strong enough to overcome any confusion created, I ordinarily tried to sharpen the measuring instruments.

Occasionally it was convenient to use "Don't Know" responses as a positive "event" of interest to the analysis. For example, some of the tentative interpretations of the saliency of status systems in Chapter 2 depend partly on sex-differences in "Don't Know" responses. And the "Ambigu-

---

5.   The hypothesis-testing model is itself only useful in scientific research when the hypotheses are derived from the theory — not when they are just empirical regularities already "verified" by sophisticated informal observation. It does make sophisticated observation easier to communicate.

ous" curriculum choices in Chapters 3 and 4 included both "Don't Know" and "No Answer" responses, as well as the "Official Don't Know" response of "General Education."

Another consideration for the problem of statistical validity is that the exploratory survey, the pre-test, and the survey analyzed in the text were all carried out on the same population. Further, this population was also observed with anthropological techniques. Thus, *if* some unknown factor differentiating the school studied from the population of interest caused the relations found, *then* the previous knowledge of the relation gained from the exploratory work would greatly increase the probability of "finding" the spurious relation in the final study. This merely exaggerates the effects of the "satisficing" model used in the analysis of the final survey, which would have the same effect.[6]

In summary, the method of analysis used to reduce com-

6. All these arguments for not making significance tests imply that the data ought to reach at least conventional levels of significance in such a large sample as this one. Conclusions ought not to be stated without qualification in the body of the work unless the supporting statistical data at least reach conventional levels. (Note that many conclusions rest on several tables, so that some combined test of all of them is legitimate.) That is, if any conclusion in this work turns out on computation to be supported to less than about the 0.05 confidence level, I have made a mistake in judgment and ought to be called to account. Most of the literature debating the usefulness of significance tests in survey analysis implicity holds that conclusions should not be accepted unless (after appropriate manipulation) they reach conventional levels, but wish to place additional restrictions on inference, so as not to accept as scientifically valuable some statistically "significant" results. See Hanan Selvin, "A Critique of Tests of Significance in Survey Research," *American Sociological Review*, Vol. 22 (October 1957), pp. 519-527, and more explicitly Leslie Kish, "Some Statistical Problems in Research Design," *Ibid.*, Vol. 24 (June 1959), pp. 328-338. The only discussion I know about why significance tests may be too strong is in S. M. Lipset, M. Trow, and J. S. Coleman, *Union Democracy* (Glencoe: The Free Press, 1956), pp. 429-432. However, this treatment mainly talks about situations for which appropriate statistical models have not yet been. built, such as tests of several derivations from the same hypothesis, and points out that an intuitively constructed model may be more powerful than an inappropriate standard model. In summary, I have no quarrel with significance tests as a minimum standard, but think it useless to compute them explicitly, unless one is working with data of a form with which he is not familiar.

putational and research labor, the selectivity of the universe sampled, and other considerations, cause the models of ordinary statistical methods to distort actual events. I have done the statistical work very informally, and have asked the reader to make both judgments of statistical significance and importance (i.e., judgments of the size of the relations) with me. Some rapid, short-cut approximations to more conventional statistical treatment, for readers who wish to apply them, are presented later in this appendix, and applied to some of the tables of the text for illustrative purposes.

In the long run, the solidity of the inferences made here will need to be checked by sampling more representative populations, by verifying the relations using other indicators, and by deduction from the theory used. It is my own conviction that the use of other indicators (e.g., juvenile delinquency) and the deduction of results in different universes (e.g., teacher turnover) will be more productive of disconfirmations of the theory than will better sampling of the adolescent population.

The basic objection to attaching much importance to significance tests is that specific hypotheses might be validated merely because I could guess the relations on the basis of observation. If this happened consistently, then the theory did not predict *any* relations not already predicted on another basis. A theory that *only* predicts already known facts gets little verification from a new demonstration of the *same* facts, collected in a slightly different way. Only previously unknown and otherwise improbable facts increase the credibility of a theory by very much.

SUMMARY OF THE MAIN
MEASURING INSTRUMENTS

The index of behavioral rebellion used in Chapter 2 consists of a partial ordering of the respondents by patterns of response to the following three items (+indicates responses considered rebellious): 1. "Which type of class did you get a flunk notice for (check as many as you got notices in, whether or not you actually flunked)?"

Negative Responses	Positive Responses
— Advanced English	+ Orientation (Freshman English and Social Studies)
— A Foreign Language	+ Social Studies (including Health)
— A Laboratory Science	+ General or Remedial English
— College Prep. Math (Algebra, Geometry, Trig)	+ General Science or General Biology
— None	+ Electronics or Conservation
— No Answer	+ General Business
	+ Basic Math, Arithmetic, or Consumer Math
	+ Any Business class except General Business
	+ Any Shop class (including Mechanical Drawing)
	+ Physical Education
	+ Any Music class
	+ Any Arts or Crafts class
	+ Agriculture or Forestry

2. "Have you ever skipped school with a gang of kids (whether or not you got caught)?"

Negative Responses	Positive Responses
— No	+ Yes
— Don't Know	
— No Answer	

3. "Have you ever been sent out of class to the Attendance Office by a teacher you didn't get along with?"

Negative Responses   *Positive Responses*
— No   + Yes
— Don't Know
— No Answer

This creates a partial ordering of eight cells. The response pattern +++, for instance, is a more rebellious response than any of the other seven possible response patterns. The patterns ++—, +—+, and —++ are each more rebellious than three other patterns. The three response patterns with only one rebellious act are all more rebellious than the ——— pattern.

These three indicators are related to each other, as can be seen from Table III. In each case, the percentages on the right are greater than the percentages on the left. That is, in every case, those rebellious by one criterion are more likely to be rebellious by another.

Further, these indicators are related to other deviant behavior. Students who are more rebellious are more likely to report having cheated or having had friends cheat for them. Among boys, for example, 46 per cent of those most rebellious by the above three indicators say they have cheated during the past month. Only 22 per cent of the well-behaved boys say they have cheated. Likewise, those who are more rebellious are much less likely than well-behaved students to do homework. Seventy-eight per cent of the most rebellious boys do less than an hour of homework outside school each day; only 35 per cent of the well-behaved boys do less than an hour's work.[7] And, as demonstrated above, students who are more rebellious by the index used here are more likely to disobey the implicit command to "Answer the question" in the interview schedule.

All the evidence, then, shows that the rebellion index taps

7. The complete tabulations of these two items against the index of rebellion show consistent patterns. Only two cells in the cheating tabulation, and only one in the homework tabulation, create differences not in the expected direction.

**Table III: Students more rebellious on one criterion are more
likely to be rebellious on others, among both boys and girls.
Data for upper classmen.**

3A: Percentage of Each Sex Who Have Skipped, Among Those Who
Have and Have Not Received Non-College Flunk Notices.

Sex	Receipt of Non-College Flunk Notice	
	No	Yes
Girls	23% (385)	45% (82)
Boys	31% (363)	52% (187)

3B: Percentage of Each Sex Who Have Been Sent Out of Class by
Receipt of Flunk Notice.

Sex	Receipt of Flunk Notice	
	No	Yes
Girls	3% (385)	11% (82)
Boys	25% (363)	45% (187)

3C: Percentage of Each Sex Who Have Skipped School with a
Group, by Classroom Discipline Record.

Sex	Have Not Been Sent Out	Have Been Sent Out
Girls	25% (447)	65% (20)
Boys	29% (375)	58% (175)

a propensity to violate the norms of the school. Further, this
propensity is diagnosed as such by the school, and there is
evidence that the school responds with disciplinary action to
the propensity measured by the rebellion index, as well as
to the behavior itself. We may consider two kinds of disciplinary action — punishment for behavior and "preventive
discipline."

Suppose that two students have each skipped school, but
one of them has also been sent out of class, while the other

has not. If the one who was sent out of class is much more likely to have been caught for his truancy (which we will demonstrate below), then there are two possibilities: (1) he has skipped more often, or (2) either he or the Attendance Office has acted in such a way as to increase his chances of being caught.

In case (1), no confusion results to our index, since the one also sent out of class has actually skipped more often, and is more behaviorally rebellious. We merely win back some precision lost in dichotomizing truancy. In case (2), if *he* acted in such a way as to be likely to be caught, then he was rebelliously *flaunting* rather than merely *evading* the attendance rules. Since flaunting is part of the complex we want to measure, it introduces no confusion either. If the Attendance Office was especially watchful of the student who had been kicked out of class, then the student in question seemed to be a special problem to the administration. If we can further demonstrate that this special watchfulness was not due to other factors,[8] then we have shown that the Attendance Office responds to the propensity measured by the index as well as to the actual behavior.

Whatever may be the causes of differential enforcement, if rebellious students (at a given level of *actual* truancy) are more likely to get into truancy trouble, then the index is measuring correctly.[9]

Table IV presents the proportion of students who have *not* come into contact with the Attendance Office for truancy, by sex and *other rebellion, among people with the same self-reported truancy record.* Table V presents the pro-

8. Since the community is ethnically homogeneous, the other factor that immediately comes to mind is social class.
9. Here, as in Chapter 3, we see that official delinquency statistics have *advantages* over statistics on actual delinquency for certain theoretical purposes, because official agencies tend to select the most rebellious of delinquent acts. If the theoretical problem concerns rebellion, rather than delinquency, then official statistics are more to the point than actual statistics.

portion of students who have not come into contact with the
Attendance Office, by sex and *social class,* among people
with the same self-reported truancy record.

Table IV: Those who have flunked or been sent out of class
are less likely to have no truancy record in the Attendance
Office, even at the same level of self-reported truancy. Percentage *never* in Attendance Office for an unexcused absence, for upper classmen.

	Self-Reported Non-Truants	
Other Rebellion	Girls	Boys
Well-Behaved	83% (293)	80% (207)
Received Flunk Notice	79% (42)	68% (60)
Sent Out of Class	*	66% (44)
Both Flunked and Sent	*	41% (29)
	Self-Reported Truants	
Well-Behaved	41% (81)	48% (66)
Received Flunk Notice	39% (31)	26% (42)
Sent Out of Class	*	30% (46)
Both Flunked and Sent	*	14% (56)

*Too few cases for meaningful percentages.

It is clear that in Table IV, the percentage caught by the
Attendance Office increases as we go down the columns;
that is, more rebellious students are more likely to encounter
truancy trouble *at a given level of truancy.* But in Table V,
there are no consistent differences by social class. Only non-
skipping girls show any social class differences in getting
into trouble. The other differences by social class are sufficiently small to be due to chance.[10]

10.   The sex differences are unlikely to be due to chance, but are
irrelevant to our present purpose.

Table V: Working class students are no more likely to have
a truancy record than middle class students, at the same
level of self-reported truancy. Percentage *never* in Attendance Office for unexcused absence.

	Self-Reported Non-Truants	
Social Class*	Girls	Boys
Middle	91% (160)	77% (137)
Working	84% (359)	77% (362)
	Self-Reported Truants	
Middle	39% (28)	34% (64)
Working	40% (109)	33% (171)

*Combined criteria of occupation of father and clothes father wears
to work. If students were middle class by either criterion, they
were classified as middle class. If they were not middle class,
they were classified as working class if they answered either
question. If they answered neither, they were omitted from the
tabulation.

That is, if prejudice exists in the Attendance Office, it is
prejudice against troublemakers rather than against working class students. It is clear that the officials were as fair
as they knew how to be, and very close to absolutely fair,
to students of different social backgrounds.[1] Any prejudice
that exists is a prejudice against students with the propensities indicated by the rebellion index, and against boys.

We discover a similar validation of our index if we consider
the proportion of students who have had their programs
changed because they didn't get along with a teacher. A

1. When Hollingshead found discrimination in enforcement by social background in Elmtown, *op. cit.*, he tentatively inferred that this
was a necessary consequence of a class system. We see from the
data above that it is not, since there is certainly a class system here,
but no discrimination *by social class* in enforcement.

change of program tends to involve the Counseling Office more than the Principal's Office, and to be "preventive" discipline. Therefore, if students with an equivalent level of self-reported classroom discipline record have different levels of program change depending on their record of non-classroom offenses, then the Counseling Office is sensitive to the propensity to rebel measured here. Table VI presents the relevant data.

Table VI: Students who have flunked or skipped school are more likely to have had their programs changed "because of a teacher [they] didn't get along with," whether they have been sent out of class or not. Percentage having program changed.

Other Rebellion	Have Not Been Sent Out	
	Girls	Boys
Well-Behaved	3% (293)	6% (207)
Received Flunk Notice	— — (42)	3% (60)
Skipped	4% (81)	9% (66)
Both Skipped and Flunked	16% (31)	26% (42)
	Have Been Sent Out	
Well-Behaved	*	23% (44)
Received Flunk Notice	*	34% (29)
Skipped	*	35% (46)
Both Skipped and Flunked	*	41% (56)

*Too few cases for meaningful percentages.

In all but two cases, those who were more rebellious by *other criteria than classroom discipline* are more likely to have had programs changed. Not only, then, is the index a measure of a syndrome of behavior which reflects non-commitment to the rules of the school. The propensities to rebel, revealed by the index, are apparently those which cause trouble for the school administration. In other words, the people who enforce school norms interpret behavioral commitment to the school in approximately the same terms as the index.

The index of age-grade orientation is likewise created out of three items (+ indicates a claim to adult rights).

1. "You really need a car of your own to have your share of fun in high school."

Negative Responses	*Positive Responses*
— Indifferent	+Strongly Agree
— Disagree	+Agree
— Strongly Disagree	
— Don't Know	
— No Answer	

2. "It's a student's own business if he wants to smoke, and the school should do away with the smoking boundaries."[2]

Negative Responses	*Positive Responses*
— Disagree	+ Strongly Agree
— Strongly Disagree	+ Agree
	+ Indifferent
	+ Don't Know
	+ No Answer

3. "What age would you say was the earliest age at which a girl ought to consider getting married, supposing that she had been asked by a man she would like to marry?"

Negative Responses	*Positive Responses*
— At least 18	+ Any time
— At least 20	+ She should be at least 16
— At least 22	
— Over 22	
— No opinion	
— No Answer	

2. "Smoking boundaries" refer to a radius around the school within which smoking by students is prohibited.

Since this approached more closely the standard criteria for fully ordinal measurement, the following patterns were selected to bear the main burden of the analysis.

	Item		
Scale No.	3. (Early Marriage)	2. (Smoking)	1. (Need Car)
1	−	−	−
2	−	−	+
3	−	+	+
4	+	+	+

Since, however, the actual strength of the measure is only a partial ordering, the error patterns were also analyzed, and given names as follows:

	Item		
Scale No.	3. (Early Marriage)	2. (Smoking)	1. (Need Car)
E1.5	−	+	−
E2	+	−	−
E3	+	−	+
E3.5	+	+	−

The numbers of the error patterns are chosen so that if a response pattern is ordered with respect to another response pattern, its number is smaller if it has fewer positive responses.

STATISTICS FOR SUMMARIZING
PARTIAL ORDERINGS

In Chapter 5 we used a set of statistics for analyzing partial orderings developed by James S. Coleman.[3] Though the model on the basis of which these statistics were developed is relatively complicated, the final estimates of parameters are intuitively easy to understand.

The best estimate of the effect of a dichotomous attribute

3.   "Multi-Variate Analysis," *op. cit.*

in a cross classification, under the assumptions of the model,[4] is the mean difference in proportion positive on the dependent variable, between cells which differ only on the attribute in question. These statistics (the mean differences for each attribute) are labeled a, b, c, and d in Chapter 5.

In addition, two parameters are derivable which give an estimate of the remaining unexplained variation (in the positive and negative directions on the dependent attribute). These are labeled "r" (for "random shock" in the positive direction) and "s" (for "random shock" in the negative direction). Intuitively speaking, these are the best estimates, under the assumptions of the model, of the proportion giving a *positive* response on the dependent variable when *none* of the independent attributes operate in a positive direction. The "s" is the best estimate of the proportion giving *negative* answers when *all* of the independent attributes operate in a positive direction. These estimates turn out to be a sort of weighted mean of the proportions in the various cells.[5]

This procedure, in effect, partitions the variation in the table. First, r equals the proportion of positive responses unexplained (the best estimate of the first cell, where none

4.   Two of the relevant assumptions are linearity (or additivity of the effects of each attribute) and equal reliability of the proportions in each of the cells. The latter assumption is not fully met by the data in Chapter 5, as some of the proportions are based on small numbers. But the overall results seem not much affected as long as the proportions are sufficiently in line to give a small number of inversions on the sign test. Since I had carried out the sign tests before I found the statistical technique used here, and since all but two of the tables in Chapter 5 showed a high degree of regularity, I have made the equal reliability assumption. (Table 40 and Table 41 are slightly unreliable.) Weighting procedures have not been satisfactorily developed, and those that exist at present greatly increase computational labor.
5.   For example, to estimate "r" in the 3 attribute case, the proportion positive in the first cell is weighted 2, the cells with one attribute encouraging a positive response are weighted 1, those with two attributes tending to cause a positive response are weighted O, and the cell with all three attributes tending toward a positive response is weighted -1. Then a "mean" is obtained by dividing by 4.

of the variables in the analysis are operating); second, a, b, c, d, (etc.) are the proportions of the variation explained by the first, second, third, fourth, and further independent attributes. When these are added together (r + a + b + c + d) we gain the best estimate of the proportion positive in the final cell, since the model assumes effects to be additive. That is, when all the variables are operating to produce a positive response, the proportion positive should be the sum of the effects of each of the variables by itself, plus unexplained effects (r) in the positive direction. The remaining variation [s = 1 − (r + a + b + c + d)] is the best estimate of proportion who give negative responses on the dependent variable when all forces work in a positive direction.

◆

TESTING THE RELATION
OF A PARTIALLY ORDERED
VARIABLE TO A DICHOTOMY

Suppose then that we classify a population by three items simultaneously, each of which we take as an indicator of a variable, but which we do not want to treat as creating a complete ordering. Then we compute the proportions positive for each of the eight cells created by these three items on some dichotomous dependent variable. The null hypothesis is that these proportions will be un-ordered. An hypothesis against which we may test this null hypothesis would be that the *proportions* were ordered in keeping with the partial ordering diagram (see Figure 5), where indicates the proportion in the cell which is positive on all three items, and so forth. If the hypothesis that we have in mind as an alternative to the null hypothesis predicts the direction of the ordering, then the problem of testing the data for significance reduces to the problem of classifying the possible permutations of the eight proportions according to their

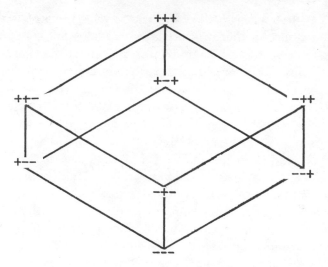

Figure 5: Partial Ordering of Response Patterns

degree of compatibility with the predicted partial orderings. One index of the degree of compatibility would be whether each of the differences between proportions had the proper sign, as predicted from the diagram. I have found no way to classify the permutations except to write them all out and check each one to see how many inversions it creates, which soon becomes tedious and is highly subject to clerical error. There seem to be forty-eight permutations of eight proportions which are completely compatible with the partial ordering diagram, and 150 permutations which produce exactly one inversion (this does not allow for ties). So there would be a probability of 198/8!, or approximately .005, of getting one or fewer inversions from the predicted order in a table with eight cells, where a partial ordering of the type outlined above is predicted.

Because of the tediousness and sheer clerical difficulty of listing permutations, particularly when some other variable or variables are controlled, and because of the low power of a sign test when the scores creating the comparisons are proportions, another approach is required. We might be willing to make a linear assumption (additivity of the effects of the items which measure the partially ordered variable), as in the Coleman model outlined above. This is essentially equivalent, for instance, to saying that the effect of claiming the right to own a car on the proportion rebellious is the same whether or not the student claims the right to smoke, and also that the effects of both smoking and of claiming the right to own a car can be meaningfully interpreted as being due to the same variable. Our estimate of each of the effects, as pointed out above, will be the average difference on an item, with everything else controlled. These are the statistics a, b, and c in Chapter 5.

With a linear assumption as outlined, the sum of the effects of all the items will be a statistic measuring the strength of the relation between the partially ordered variable and the dichotomy. In Chapter 5 the statistic a + b + c in the text near Table 35 and below Tables 36 through 41 is such a measure. Because such a statistic is a linear combination of the proportions in the various cells, the proportions in the cells having a binomial distribution which is approximately normal, the sampling distribution of this statistic is also approximately normal and may be computed according to the method developed by Goodman.[6]

6.   If a statistic is a linear combination of n proportions $\sum\limits_{i=1}^{n} a_i p_i$, where the a_i are the coefficients of the proportions and the p_i are the proportions, then the sample statistic has an approximately normal distribution with a mean equal to the statistic and a variance equal to

$$\sum_{i=1}^{n} a_i^2 \frac{p_i(1-p_i)}{N_i}$$

where N_i is the number of cases on which p_i is based. Cf. Leo Goodman, "Modifications of the Dorn-Stouffer-Tibbetst Method for 'Testing the Significance of Comparisons in Sociological Data,'" *American Journal of Sociology*, Vol. 66, No. 4, pp. 355-363. Or see Anders Hald, *Statistical Theory with Engineering Applications* (New York: John Wiley, 1952), pp. 676-685, 125, 214-216, and 117-118.

Thus, for example, the standard error of a + b + c in Table 35 of Chapter 5 is a little more than 6 per cent, which gives for that table a z-score of the sum of more than 7.00, which is of course very improbable under the null hypothesis. The computations of these standard errors are sufficiently tedious (involving computing the estimated variance for each proportion in the table) as not to be generally worthwhile. For the tables in Chapter 5 where the statistic a + b + c is given, the standard error of this sum will be less than .07. Since in each case the theory gives a prediction of the sign of this sum, the appropriate test is one-tailed. In general then, the sum will be significant at the .01 level if it is greater than about .16 (*i.e.*, 2.33 x .07). Thus Tables 36 through 41 of Chapter 5 are clearly significant at the .01 level.

For the tables in Chapter 2, a statistic would have to be computed to take account of the fact that some of the cells (those made up of girls who have been sent out of class) do not have sufficient cases. The effects of each item of the rebellion index can be estimated by averaging those percentage differences not involving the virtually empty cells. The sum of these estimated effects will be also a linear combination of the proportions in all the filled cells, with coefficients depending on which cells have too few cases. In the tables of Chapter 2, then, there are six estimates of the relation between cutting school and the dichotomous variables (two among girls, four among boys) and the same number for flunk notices, but only four estimates, all among boys, of the relation to being sent out of class. The distribution of such a statistic may be derived as before. For instance, the estimate of a + b + c (the sum of the relations of the rebellion items to the perception that parents would feel uncomfortable around the school) for the weak relation reported in Table 9 of Chapter 2 is about .16, while the standard error of this sum is a little less than .07. This gives a z-score of more than 2.33, and a probability on a one-tailed basis of less than .01.

But, as can easily be seen from inspection of the table, a linear model does not fit these data very well, for the relation is quite strong among girls and weak among boys. This, in turn, is theoretically meaningful and similar to certain other results, as explained in the text. Where there is substantial reason to believe that a linear model does not fit well, it is not wise to use a statistic which assumes such a model. Though we could derive appropriate statistics to assess the degree of confidence with which we can assert the intuitively obvious from the table (namely that there probably is a positive relation among girls, that the relation among boys may be due to sampling fluctuations, but that if there is a relation among boys it is very likely positive) the gain would scarcely be worth the effort.[7]

But here it is even somewhat tedious to work out the exact expression for the sum of the effects, let alone all the different variances, so a device for saving computational labor may be proposed. It will be remembered that the sum a+b+c is a best estimate, using all the data, of the difference between the cell in which all three items are positive, and that in which all are negative. Of course, another estimate of this difference is the empirically obtained difference between the first and the last cell. This estimate will often have more error, but can be used whenever the numbers in each of the extreme cells are reasonably large. Thus it would be reasonable to use the difference between the first and last cell for boys in the tables in Chapter 2, where the case bases are respectively 207 and 56, but not for girls, where the case base of the most rebellious cell is only 6.

Let us take, for example, the relations of rebellion to other

7. Using the appropriate statistic for boys alone, the estimate of a+b+c is about .12, with a standard error of a little more than .07, for a z-score of 1.66. On a one-tailed basis this is just significant at .05, which is quite unreliable from the point of view of this study. The method for testing a relation of a partially ordered variable and a dichotomy proposed in my dissertation, on which this book is based, is invalid. It involved treating each comparison between proportions, for which the partial ordering made possible a prediction of direction, as an independent sign test. These sign tests are not independent.

variables for boys reported in Chapter 2. The standard error of the difference between the extreme cells (*i.e.*, the well-behaved and the most rebellious boys) will be

$$\sqrt{\frac{p_1(1-p_1)}{N_1} + \frac{p_8(1-p_8)}{N_8}} \; .$$

With N_1 and N_8 (the case bases in the first and last cell) given, this will be at a maximum when both p_1 and p_8 (the proportions in the first and last cell) equal .50. So the upper limit of the standard error will be

$$\sqrt{\frac{.25}{N_1} + \frac{.25}{N_8}} = \frac{1}{2}\sqrt{\frac{1}{N_1} + \frac{1}{N_8}} \; .$$

The upper limit of the standard error for the relations between rebellion and other variables, for boys (in the bottom half of the tables in Chapter 2) will be this function evaluated at $N_1 = 207$, $N_8 = 56$, or about .076. Since a one-tailed test is appropriate in these tables, we will be conservative if we say that any difference between the extreme cells for boys will be significant at .01 if the difference is greater than or equal to 18 per cent ($2.33 \times .076$).

Since all the relations between rebellion and the attitude questions for boys in Chapter 2 are significant at the .01 level by this conservative test, except that in Table 9 (which was analyzed above and found to be significant for boys at .05, and for the whole sample at .01), there is no point in computing the exact statistic $a + b + c$ unless it is of substantive interest to estimate its size, nor in computing the exact standard error of the statistic unless we want that estimate in the form of a confidence interval. Since there is no reason to believe that the measures used in this study are likely to become standard research tools and to be applied to other populations in exactly the form used here, it seems that such estimates would not be of scientific value. They would be useful only to aid in an intuitive judgment of whether the relations are "big" or "unimportant," and these judgments do not really need such complicated paraphernalia.

Appendix II:
The Survey Schedule

STUDY OF STUDENT ATTITUDES

This questionnaire is part of a study being carried on at the University of California, of students' attitudes toward high school and toward their careers. All questionnaires will be analyzed statistically, and no names or other identification of students will be used. Your teachers will not look at your questionnaire or find out how you answered. You need not put your name on this questionnaire.

This is an attitude questionnaire, not a test; there are no right and wrong answers. Disregard the numbers on the extreme right. They are to help us tabulate the answers at the university. Please check only one answer to each question, unless there are directions to do otherwise. Try to answer every question. Do not spend very much time on any one question.

(Put a check mark
on the proper line)

1

1. Year in school?

Freshman _____ -1
Sophomore _____ -2
Junior _____ -3
Senior _____ -4

2

2. Age at last birthday?

11 _____ -1
12 _____ -2
13 _____ -3
14 _____ -4
15 _____ -5
16 _____ -6
17 _____ -7
18 _____ -8
19 _____ -9
20 or more _____ -0

214

3. What freshman math class did you take? (If you are a   3
freshman, which are you taking now?)

Arithmetic _____ -1
General or Basic Math _____ -2
General Business _____ -3
Algebra _____ -4
None _____ -5

4. Please check the English class you are now taking.*

Freshmen   Sophomores

                                                                  4

Remedial Reading   ___ -1   Remedial Reading II___ -1
Remedial English   ___ -2   Remedial English II___ -2
Any other Orientation___ -3   General English   II___ -3
                                Advanced English II___ -4

Juniors   Seniors

Remedial Reading III ___ -1
Remedial English III ___ -2
General English III ___ -3   General English   IV___ -3
Advanced English III ___ -4   Advanced English IV___ -4
Honors English III ___ -5   Honors English   IV___ -5
                                No English   ___ -6

*Remedial and honors classes were identified by the
names of the teachers, which have been omitted here.

5. Have you ever received a notice from the counseling
office for flunking a class or doing poor work in a class?   5

Yes _____ -1
No _____ -2
Don't know _____ -3

6. Which type of class did you get a flunk notice for?
(Check as many as you got notices in, whether or not
you actually flunked.)   6

Advanced English _____ -1
A Foreign Language _____ -1
A Laboratory Science _____ -1

(question 6 continued)   6

College Prep Math _____ -1
(algebra, geometry, trig)
Orientation _____ -2
Social Studies _____ -2
(including Health)
General or Remedial English _____ -2
General Science or Gen. Biol. _____ -2
Electronics or Conservation _____ -2
General Business _____ -2
Basic math, Arithmetic, or Consumer math _____ -2

Any business class except General Business _____ -3

Any Shop class _____ -4
(Including Mechanical Drawing)

Physical Education _____ -5

Any Home Economics class _____ -6

Any Music class _____ -7

Any Arts or Crafts class _____ -8

Agriculture or Forestry _____ -9

None _____ -0

7. What would you say was your average grade in
high school subjects?   7

Mostly A's _____ -1
Mixed A's and B's _____ -2
Mostly B's _____ -3
Mixed B's and C's _____ -4
Mostly C's _____ -5
Mixed C's and D's _____ -6
Mostly D's _____ -7
Mixed D's and F's _____ -8
Mostly F's _____ -9
Don't Know _____ -0

8. How many times have you been into the
   Attendance Office for an **Unexcused** Absence?   8

   Never _____ -1
   Once or Twice _____ -2
   3 or 4 Times _____ -3
   More Than 4 Times _____ -4
   Don't Know _____ -5

9. Have you ever skipped school with a gang of
   kids (whether or not you got caught?)   9

   Yes _____ -1
   No _____ -2
   Don't Know _____ -3

10. Have you ever been sent out of class to the
    Attendance Office by a teacher you didn't get along with?   10

    Yes _____ -1
    No _____ -2
    Don't Know _____ -3

11. Have you ever had your program changed because
    you didn't get along with a teacher?   11

    Yes _____ -1
    No _____ -2
    Don't Know _____ -3

12. What curriculum are you **most** interested in in
    high school? (Please check only one answer.)   12

    Vocational Industrial Arts _____ -1
    General Education _____ -2
    College Preparatory _____ -3
    Vocational Agriculture _____ -4
    Business Education _____ -5
    Don't Know _____ -6

13. What type of job would you like most of all to be
    doing ten years from now?   13

    Skilled worker (for instance,
    plumber, machinist, auto mechanic) _____ -1
    Entertainer _____ -2

(question 13 continued)   13

Clerical or secretarial work _____ -3
Sales clerk or salesman _____ -4
Professional work (for instance,
doctor, lawyer, teacher, engineer) _____ -5
In a small business for yourself _____ -6
Farm Owner or worker _____ -7
Housewife _____ -8
A good paying job in a mill,
factory, or in the woods _____ -9
Other (What? _____)
Don't Know _____ -0

14. What sort of job do you think you will probably
really have ten years from now?   14

Skilled worker _____ -1
Entertainer _____ -2
Clerical or Secretarial _____ -3
Sales Clerk or Salesman _____ -4
Professional work _____ -5
Small business for yourself _____ -6
Farm owner or worker _____ -7
Housewife _____ -8
A job in a mill, factory, or woods _____ -9
Other (What? _____)
Don't Know _____ -0

15. Have you **definitely decided** whether or not to go
to college?   15

Definitely decided to go _____ -1
Definitely decided **not** to go _____ -2
Not decided _____ -3
Don't Know _____ -4

16. (If you are not decided, or don't know, answer this
question.) What do you think you probably will do,
go to college or not?   16

Probably **will** go _____ -1
Probably will **not** go _____ -2
Don't Know _____ -3

17. Do your parents urge you to go to college and to
take college preparatory subjects in high school?   17

                  Yes, strongly urge _____ -1
            Yes, moderately urge _____ -2
      No, leave it to my own decision _____ -3
        No, urge me to get a job _____ -4
                  Don't Know _____ -5

18. If you could be any of these things you wanted, which
would you most want to be? (Answer only if male.)   18

                       Jet Pilot _____ -1
        Nationally famous athlete _____ -2
                 Missionary _____ -3
             Atomic Scientist _____ -4

19. How many of your subjects this year would you
say were **pretty boring?**   19

                    All boring _____ -1
        Only one or two interesting _____ -2
            About half and half _____ -3
          Only one or two boring _____ -4
               All interesting _____ -5
          Varies too much to say _____ -6
                  Don't Know _____ -7

20. What is your opinion on the **amount of homework**
given in your classes?   20

          Too much homework given _____ -1
        About the right amount given _____ -2
     More homework should be given _____ -3
                  Don't Know _____ -4

21. How much time, on the average, do you spend
doing homework outside school?   21

             None or almost none _____ -1
         Less than 1/2 hour a day _____ -2
           About 1/2 hour a day _____ -3
             About 1 hour a day _____ -4
        About 1-1/2 hours a day _____ -5
          About 2 hours a day _____ -6
         3 or more hours a day _____ -7

22. Suppose you had an extra hour in school and could
either take some course of your own choosing, or
use it for athletics or some other activity, or use
it for study hall. How would you use it?   22

Course _____ -1
Athletics _____ -2
Club or activity _____ -3
Study hall, to study _____ -4
Study hall, to do something else _____ -5

23. How important would you say your getting good
grades was to your parents?   23

Very important _____ -1
Quite important _____ -2
Somewhat important _____ -3
Not very important _____ -4
No importance at all _____ -5
Don't Know _____ -6

24. How important would you say your grades were to
getting the kind of job you want?   24

Very important _____ -1
Quite important _____ -2
Somewhat important _____ -3
Not very important _____ -4
No importance at all _____ -5
Don't Know _____ -6

25. How important would you say your grades were to
your own satisfaction?   25

Very important _____ -1
Quite important _____ -2
Somewhat important _____ -3
Not very important _____ -4
No importance at all _____ -5
Don't Know _____ -6

26. Have you personally cheated on any assignment or
test or in reporting your grade, or have any of your
friends cheated for you when correcting one of
your tests, **during the past month?**   26

Yes, I have cheated _____ -1

Yes, friend cheated for me _____ -2

No, neither _____ -3

Don't Know _____ -4

27. Do you date?   27

No _____ -1

Yes, about once a month _____ -2

Yes, once every 2 or 3 weeks _____ -3

Yes, about once a week _____ -4

Yes, about twice a week _____ -5

Yes, about three or four times a week _____ -6

Yes, more than four times a week _____ -7

28. Do you own a car? (If you are part owner of a car,
check Yes.)   28

Yes _____ -1

No _____ -2

29. Do you plan to get a car of your own **before you
get out of high school?**   29

Yes _____ -1

No _____ -2

Don't Know _____ -3

Would you strongly agree, agree, are you indifferent,
do you disagree, or strongly disagree with the following
statements?

30. You really need a car of your own to have your
share of fun in high school.   30

Strongly agree _____ -1

Agree _____ -2

Indifferent _____ -3

Disagree _____ -4

Strongly disagree _____ -5

Don't Know _____ -6

31. It's a student's own business if he wants to smoke, and the school should do away with the smoking boundaries.   31

Strongly agree _____ -1
Agree _____ -2
Indifferent _____ -3
Disagree _____ -4
Strongly disagree _____ -5
Don't Know _____ -6

32. In getting a good job, how you look is generally more important than what you can do.   32

Strongly agree _____ -1
Agree _____ -2
Indifferent _____ -3
Disagree _____ -4
Strongly disagree _____ -5
Don't Know _____ -6

33. Teachers should give good grades for neatness on themes and assignments, as well as knowledge of the subject.   33

Strongly agree _____ -1
Agree _____ -2
Indifferent _____ -3
Disagree _____ -4
Strongly disagree _____ -5
Don't Know _____ -6

34. Teachers have a right to expect cleanliness and neatness in dress, and should enforce this by basing grades partly on personal neatness.   34

Strongly agree _____ -1
Agree _____ -2
Indifferent _____ -3
Disagree _____ -4
Strongly disagree _____ -5
Don't Know _____ -6

35. Teachers generally respect a polite person who
does poor work in a class more than a good
student who is impolite.   35

Strongly agree _____ -1

Agree _____ -2

Indifferent _____ -3

Disagree _____ -4

Strongly disagree _____ -5

Don't Know _____ -6

The following statements have been made about some
schools at various times. Do you think they are Certainly
true, Probably true, Probably false, or Certainly false,
about your high school?

36. A small group of students run the activities and the
student government, and you can't do anything
unless you're in with them.   36

Certainly true _____ -1

Probably true _____ -2

Probably false _____ -3

Certainly false _____ -4

Don't Know _____ -5

37. Coaches and supervisors of student activities
play favorites.   37

Certainly true _____ -1

Probably true _____ -2

Probably false _____ -3

Certainly false _____ -4

Don't Know _____ -5

38. You have to get in good with the teachers if you
expect to get a fair grade in this school.   38

Certainly true _____ -1

Probably true _____ -2

Probably false _____ -3

Certainly false _____ -4

Don't Know _____ -5

39. It doesn't matter very much how hard you work in a class — your grade is pretty much set when you first come in.

        39

                  Certainly true _____ -1
                  Probably true _____ -2
                  Probably false _____ -3
                  Certainly false _____ -4
                  Don't Know _____ -5

40. One thing wrong with this school is that a lot of students don't behave themselves well enough.

        40

                  Certainly true _____ -1
                  Probably true _____ -2
                  Probably false _____ -3
                  Certainly false _____ -4
                  Don't Know _____ -5

41. One thing wrong with this school is the number of "squares" among the students, who would rather follow all the rules than have any fun.

        41

                  Certainly true ✓ -1
                  Probably true _____ -2
                  Probably false _____ -3
                  Certainly false _____ -4
                  Don't Know _____ -5

42. Most parents would feel uncomfortable coming to see a teacher or to a PTA meeting.

        42

                  Certainly true _____ -1
                  Probably true _____ -2
                  Probably false _____ -3
                  Certainly false _____ -4
                  Don't Know _____ -5

43. The Attendance Office is out to get certain people, more than to apply the rules fairly.

        43

                  Certainly true _____ -1
                  Probably true _____ -2
                  Probably false _____ -3
                  Certainly false _____ -4
                  Don't Know   -5

Personal Attitudes

What is your reaction to the following situation?

A group of 10 boys form a club. They all decide to go to San Francisco to some auto races. It will cost about $11.00 a boy. They all get jobs and save their money for a while. When the time of the races comes, they all have their money except one boy who is broke. One of his friends has earned and saved some extra money and says, "I'll pay your way." But the boy without the money says, "No, you worked hard and saved the money. The money is yours and I have no right to it." The other boy says, "Yes, but you're my friend, and friends are supposed to help one another. I'll pay your way. Even if you can't pay me back, that's OK."

44. Do you think the boy who was broke could find a way to pay back the money to his friend if he really tried?   44

Yes, certainly could _____ -1

Probably could _____ -2

Might not be able to _____ -3

45. Suppose you were the boy who was broke, and you had just been laid off from your job and didn't know where you could get another. Would you let your friend pay your way if he really wanted you to go with the gang?   45

Would let him pay _____ -1

Would not let him pay _____ -2

Depends on how good a friend he was _____ -3

Don't Know _____ -4

46. How hard was it to make up your mind on the last question (question 45)?   46

Very hard _____ -1

Quite hard _____ -2

Quite easy _____ -3

No trouble at all _____ -4

Don't Know _____ -5

47. When a new clothing style comes out, how soon do
    you change to the new style?   47
        1. I'm usually one of the first in my group
                                    to change _____ -1
        2. I change about the same time that most
                            other people in my group change _____ -2
    — 3. I usually don't change until most of my
                            friends have changed _____ -3
        4. I don't follow the change at all _____ -4
        5. Clothing styles don't matter to me _____ -5

48-52. Rank the five items below in terms of their
       importance to you on a job.   48-52
                                    (Rank from 1 to 5) (col.)
                    The security of steady work _____ 48
                    The opportunity for a rapid rise _____ 49
                    The enjoyment of the work itself _____ 50
                    Friendly people to work with _____ 51
                                    A high income _____ 52

53-56. Different people strive for different things.
       Here are some things that you have probably
       thought about. Among the things you strive
       for during your high school days, just how
       important is each of these?   53-56
                                    (Rank from 1 to 4) (col.)
                            Pleasing my parents _____ 53
                Learning as much as possible in school _____ 54
                    Living up to my religious ideals _____ 55
            Being accepted and liked by other students _____ 56

57. If you could be remembered here at school for one
    of the three things below, which one would you
    want it to be?   57
                                    Brilliant student _____ -1
                                    Athletic star _____ -2
                                    Most popular _____ -3

58. What age would you say was the earliest age at
which a girl ought to consider getting married,
supposing that she had been asked by a man she
would like to marry?   58

Any time _____ -1

She should be at least 16 _____ -2

At least 18 _____ -3

At least 20 _____ -4

At least 22 _____ -5

Over 22 _____ -6

No opinion _____ -7

59. One student said, "I would feel embarrassed to
bring some kids I know at school home to stay
over a weekend." Have you ever felt you would
be embarrassed to bring any student you have met
home with you?   59

Have felt that way _____ -1

Have never felt that way _____ -2

Can't recall _____ -3

The following questions are to furnish information for statistical purposes, for comparing attitudes of different students.

60. Where do you live now?   60

Within [the town's] city limits _____ -1

Just outside [the town] (for instance, [a town]) _____ -2

In a small town some distance from [the town]
(for instance, [other towns]) _____ -3

Out in the country _____ -4

Other (Where? _____)

61. How long have you lived in this school district?   61

Came during this school year _____ -1

Came since entering high school,
but before this year _____ -2

Came during grade school or junior high _____ -3

Came before entering grade school _____ -4

Lived here since birth _____ -5

Don't know _____ -6

62. (If you **moved to** this area since birth, answer this question.) What part of the country did you live in **just before** you came to this area?   62

Another place in California _____ -1
Oregon or Washington _____ -2
The "Border" states (Ky., Ark., Tenn., Mo., Okla., Texas, Md.) _____ -3
The Deep South _____ -4
The Rocky Mountain States _____ -5
The Midwest _____ -6
New England or Middle Atlantic _____ -7
Outside the U.S. _____ -8

63. Do you live with both your parents, with one of them alone, one of them and a stepparent, or with neither of them?   63

Both parents _____ -1
Mother alone _____ -2
Father alone _____ -3
Mother and Stepfather _____ -4
Father and Stepmother _____ -5
Neither mother nor father _____ -6

64. How many brothers and sisters do you have (**not** counting yourself)?   64

None _____ -0
One _____ -1
Two _____ -2
Three _____ -3
Four _____ -4
Five _____ -5
Six _____ -6
Seven _____ -7
Eight or more _____ -8

65. Is your father (or stepfather) working now?   65

Working _____ -1
Unemployed _____ -2
Not living with Father or Stepfather _____ -3
Don't know _____ -4

66. What sort of work does your father (or stepfather) do?
(If he is retired or dead, what sort of work did he
generally do when working?)   66

   1. Professional work (requiring college, such as
doctor, lawyer, teacher, accountant, engineer) _____-1

   2. Owns or manages a business (for instance,
small sawmill, store, filling station, construction)   _____-2

   3. Works as a salesman or salesclerk (such as
insurance or real estate salesman, furniture
salesman, farm or logging equipment salesman) _____-3

   4. Works in an office doing clerical, secretarial,
or similar work (for instance, timekeeper, bank
teller, stock clerk, or work behind a desk)_____-4

   5. Skilled worker or foreman (for example, carpenter, plumber, millwright, machinist, auto me-
chanic, foreman in the mill or in the woods)_____-5

   6. Mill or factoryworker, truck driver, cat driver,
logging worker, or similar semi-skilled work _____-6

   7. Service worker (for instance, gas station attendant, janitor, barber, bartender or waiter)_____-7

   8. Works for a government agency as an official
(city, state, or federal, with people under him) _____-8

   9. Works for a government agency as a mailman,
fireman, policeman, repairing roads, etc.   _____-9

  10. Farmer or farm worker   _____-0

  11. Other, or can't decide which   _____-X

67. What kind of clothes does your father's (or stepfather's) job make him wear?   67

                 Relatively dressed up (for example, shirt
and tie; suit or sports jacket) _____-1

A uniform _____-2

Work clothes _____-3

Don't know _____-4

68. Does your mother have a job outside the home?   68

                                Yes, full time _____ -1

                               Yes, part time _____ -2

                                       No _____ -3

       Not living with mother or stepmother _____ -4

69. Do you belong to any school clubs?   69

                                      Yes _____ -1

                                      No _____ -2

                               Don't know _____ -3

70. Sex?   70

                                    Male _____ -1

                                Female _____ -2

Bibliography of Works Cited

(*Roman Numerals Indicate Chapter Where First Cited*)

Katherine Archibald, *Wartime Shipyard* (Berkeley: University of California Press, 1947), VI.

Howard S. Becker, "The Teacher in the Authority System of the Public School," *Journal of Educational Sociology*, Vol. 27 (November 1953), pp. 128-141, II.

Claude Bernard, *Introduction to the Study of Experimental Medicine* (New York: Dover, 1957), VII.

B. Bernstein, "Some Sociological Determinants of Perception," *British Journal of Sociology*, Vol. 9 (June 1958), pp. 159-174, III.

Garret Birkhoff and Saunders MacLane, *A Survey of Modern Algebra* (rev. ed.) (New York: MacMillan, 1953), Appendix on Method.

Robert Blauner, "Attitudes Toward Work: A Discussion of Research," in Walter Galenson and Seymour M. Lipset, eds., *Labor and Trade Unionism* (New York: John Wiley, 1960), pp. 339-360, III.

Herbert Blumer, "Race Prejudice as a Sense of Group Position," *Pacific Sociological Review,* Vol. 1 (Spring 1958), pp. 3-7, III.

Anton Chekhov, *Selected Letters of Anton Chekhov,* ed. by Lillian Hellman (New York: Farrar, Straus, 1955), VII.

Albert K. Cohen, *Delinquent Boys* (Glencoe: The Free Press, 1955), I.

———, "Social Disorganization and Deviant Behavior," in Robert K. Merton, *et al.,* eds., *Sociology Today* (New York: Basic Books, 1959), I.

James S. Coleman, *Introduction to Mathematical Sociology* (New York: Free Press, 1964).

Richard S. Crutchfield, "Conformity and Character," *American Psychologist,* Vol. 10 (May 1955), pp. 191-198, VI.

Norman Dennis, F. Henriques, and C. Slaughter, *Coal Is Our Life* (London: Eyre and Spottiswood, 1956), III.

Peter Drucker, *Concept of the Corporation* (New York: John Day, 1945), III.

S. N. Eisenstadt, *From Generation to Generation* (Glencoe: The Free Press, 1956), III.

Henry Elkin, "Aggressive and Erotic Tendencies in Army Life," *"American Journal of Sociology,* Vol. 51 (March 1946), pp. 408-413, VI.

Erik H. Erikson, *Childhood and Society* (London: Imago, n.d.), V.

———, "The Problem of Ego Identity," *Journal of the American Psychoanalytic Association,* Vol. 4 (January 1956), V.

Nelson Foote, "Identification as the Basis for a Theory of Motivation," *American Sociological Review,* Vol. 16 (1951), pp. 14-21, I.

William H. Form and Gregory P. Stone, *The Social Significance of Clothing in Occupational Life,* Technical Bulletin 247 (East Lansing: Michigan State University, 1955), VI.

Leo Goodman, "Modifications of the Dorn-Stouffer-Tibbetts

Method for 'Testing the Significance of Comparisons in Sociological Data,' " *American Journal of Sociology,* Vol. 66 (January 1961), pp. 355-363, Appendix on Method.

Anders Hald, *Statistical Theory with Engineering Applications* (New York: John Wiley, 1952), Appendix on Method.

Norman S. Hayner, "Taming the Lumberjack," *American Sociological Review,* Vol. 10 (April 1945), pp. 217-225, VI.

Richard Hoggart, *The Uses of Literacy* (London: Chatto and Windus, 1957), III.

August B. Hollingshead, *Elmtown's Youth* (New York: John Wiley, 1949), II.

Joseph A. Kahl, "Educational and Occupational Aspirations of 'Common Man' Boys," *Harvard Educational Review,* Vol. 23 (1953), VI.

Alfred C. Kinsey, et al., "Social Level and Sexual Outlet," in Reinhard Bendix and S. M. Lipset, *Class, Status, and Power* (Glencoe: The Free Press, 1953), V.

Leslie Kish, "Some Statistical Problems in Research Design," *American Sociological Review,* Vol. 24 (June 1959), pp. 328-338, Appendix on Method.

John I. Kitsuse and David C. Dietricke, "Delinquent Boys: A Critique," *American Sociological Review,* Vol. 24 (April 1959), pp. 208-215, I.

Seymour M. Lipset and Reinhard Bendix, *Social Mobility in Industrial Society* (Berkeley: University of California Press, 1959), III.

S. M. Lipset, M. Trow, and J. S. Coleman, *Union Democracy* (Glencoe: The Free Press, 1956), Appendix on Method.

T. H. Marshall, *Class, Citizenship, and Social Development* (New York: Doubleday and Co., 1964), VII.

Robert K. Merton, "Social Structure and Anomie," *Social Theory and Social Structure* (Glencoe: The Free Press, 1949), I.

F. Ivan Nye, *Family Relationships and Delinquent Behavior* (New York: John Wiley, 1958), I.

Fritz Redl and David Wineman, *Children Who Hate* (Glencoe: The Free Press, 1951), I.

———, *Controls from Within* (Glencoe: The Free Press, 1952), V.

Leonard Reissman, "Levels of Aspiration and Social Classs," *American Sociological Review*, Vol. 18 (June 1953), pp. 233-242, III.

Natalie Rogoff, "College, Careers and Social Contexts," (Paper presented at meetings of the American Sociological Society, September 1959), IV.

Louis Schneider and Sverre Lysgaard, "The Deferred Gratification Pattern: A Preliminary Study," *American Sociological Review,* Vol. 18 (April 1953), pp. 142-149, III.

Hanan Selvin, "A Critique of Tests of Significance in Survey Research," *American Sociological Review*, Vol. 23 (August 1958), pp. 519-527, Appendix on Method.

Herbert Simon, *Models of Man: Social and Rational* (New York: John Wiley, 1957), Appendix on Method.

Arthur L. Stinchcombe, "Some Social Supports of Professional Attitudes Among Construction Workers," (Paper presented at meetings of the American Sociological Society, September 1959), III.

———, "Bureaucratic and Craft Administration of Production," *Adminstrative Science Quarterly*, Vol. 3 (September 1959), pp. 168-187, III.

Lloyd Street, an unpublished study on the status of Negroes in Berkeley, California, III.

Edwin H. Sutherland, *The Professional Thief* (Chicago: University of Chicago Press, 1937), III.

——— and D. R. Cressey, *Principles of Criminology* (5th ed.) (Philadelphia: Lippincott, 1955), I.

Max Weber, *From Max Weber: Essays in Sociology* (New York: Oxford University Press, 1946), III.

————, *The Theory of Social and Economic Organization* (Glencoe: The Free Press, 1947), I.

William F. Whyte, "A Slum Sex Code," *American Journal of Sociology*, Vol. 49 (July 1943), pp. 24-31, VI.

Index

QUADRANGLE PAPERBACKS

American History

European History

William Sheridan Allen. *The Nazi Seizure of Power.* (QP302)
W. O. Henderson. *The Industrial Revolution in Europe.* (QP303)
Raul Hilberg. *The Destruction of the European Jews.* (QP301)
Telford Taylor. *Sword and Swastika.* (QP304)

Philosophy

F. H. Bradley. *The Presuppositions of Critical History.* (QP108)
William Earle. *Objectivity.* (QP109)
James M. Edie, James P. Scanlan, Mary-Barbara Zeldin, George L. Kline. *Russian Philosophy.*
    (3 vols, QP111, 112, 113)
James M. Edie. *An Invitation to Phenomenology.* (QP103)
James M. Edie. *Phenomenology in America.* (QP105)
Manfred S. Frings. *Heidegger and the Quest for Truth.* (QP107)
Moltke S. Gram. *Kant: Disputed Questions.* (QP104)
Lionel Rubinoff. *Faith and Reason.* (QP106)
Paul Tibbetts. *Perception.* (QP110)
Pierre Thévenaz. *What Is Phenomenology?* (QP101)

Social Science

George and Eunice Grier. *Equality and Beyond.* (QP204)
Charles O. Lerche, Jr. *Last Chance in Europe.* (QP207)
David Mitrany. *A Working Peace System.* (QP205)
Martin Oppenheimer and George Lakey. *A Manual for Direct Action.* (QP202)
Fred Powledge. *To Change a Child.* (QP209)
Lee Rainwater. *And the Poor Get Children.* (QP208)
Clarence Senior. *The Puerto Ricans.* (QP201)
Arthur L. Stinchcombe. *Rebellion in a High School.* (QP211)